Mastering Authentic CREPES & GALETTES

Mastering Authentic CREPES & GALETTES

Bertrand Larcher
Founder of Breizh Café

Robert ROSE

Crepes and Galettes: Step by Step

The Classic Recipes

Spring Recipes

Summer Recipes

Fall Recipes

Winter Recipes

Le Comptoir
BREIZH Ca

ECOLE
INTERNATIONALE
DE CREPIER

HARPE NOIRE
TRADITION BRETONNE
Farine
de
Blé Noir
de
Bretagne

Atelier de la Crêpe

After opening restaurants and shops that reflected the culinary culture of my region, Brittany, I opened Atelier de la Crêpe in November 2018. I had been thinking about it for years. I wanted to move into the phase of sharing my knowledge. My parents, who were farmers, handed down to me the value of work and love of good things. On the farm, we were fairly self-sufficient. We grew all our fruits and vegetables and raised all the animals ourselves: pigs, cows, chickens and goats. At the table, everything was fresh and delicious. I learned that, without the humble and patient work on the land, there can be no authentic cuisine. Later, my experience in Japan reinforced my convictions: Breton culinary culture has a strong identity and travels really well as long as its expertise is respected. Although Breizh Café was always the vehicle for this belief, it was within Atelier de la Crêpe that it fully came to take shape, through sharing.

This international school, which specializes in learning the trade of the crepe maker, or crêpier, and features a teaching restaurant, is located in Saint-Malo, on quay Duguay-Trouin. It welcomes, for six-week training sessions, interns who are interested in making this their career. It happens in 6,500 square feet in a former boathouse. The theoretical knowledge is offered upstairs, in a conference room. On the ground floor, the restaurant (which seats 70 people) is bright and elegant, furnished with light wood. Beauty and fine foods intertwine: the food products displayed on the shelves — flours, ciders, honey, jams — also have a decorative purpose. At the back, the large

At Atelier de la Crêpe, quay Duguay-Trouin, in Saint-Malo.

kitchen opens directly onto the dining room. From the dining room, you can see the Billigs (crepe-making machines) where interns, guided by our instructors, are introduced to the art of turning crepes. Teaching kitchen, restaurant kitchen: I wanted the two to blend into each other. That's the strength of this workshop. Students have to get a sense of the feelings they elicit in customers when their plates are carried into the restaurant. Amid an intense and welcoming hive of activity, the delicious smell of cooked butter wafts through the space.

This place strongly evokes our regional identity and radiates values that I wanted to breathe into it: conviviality, hospitality, local products, local distribution channels. For me, it's an ecological and social commitment. Beyond showcasing the craft, my goal is to keep the flame alive, to evoke emotions.

My career has been made up of encounters and travel. I learned a lot, I was given a lot and now I want to share that. For me, creating this workshop is a civic act. It corresponds to two of my primary motivations: giving others the desire to enter this profession and spreading the culture of taste as widely as possible.

Bertrand Larcher,
founder and brand manager,
BREIZH CAFÉ and ATELIER DE LA CRÊPE

Bertrand Larcher: A Portrait

FOUNDER OF BREIZH CAFÉ AND ATELIER DE LA CRÊPE

Crepe ambassador, Breton buckwheat pioneer in Japan, cooking entrepreneur without borders: over the years, Bertrand Larcher has acquired a unique reputation. Born on a farm near Fougères, in France, he is still a farmer at heart and has always kept in close touch with the land. Thanks to his farm upbringing, he has high standards when it comes to the quality of products and a deep respect for those who grow them. He chose to express these standards through his passion for cooking: after leaving hotel school in Dinard, he worked for a while at Harry's Bar in Geneva before following his wife, Yuko, to Japan.

There, he discovered an ancient buckwheat culture – soba, mainly in the form of noodles – but realized that there were no Breton crepe restaurants. That is how the Breizh Café concept was born. It's a creperie with many variations to choose from, built on solid principles: the excellence of farm products and traditional expertise, expressed through two main themes – buckwheat and cider.

Breizh Café, which is more than a restaurant, is a cultural and social project, a bridge between farm producers and the public. With Bertrand, the foundation of a simple and pared-down Breton cuisine is enhanced by Japanese elements. He built on the concept by constantly refreshing it: creperies in Japan, Paris and Brittany; deli counters; buckwheat house; Japanese restaurant; izakaya (sake bar); cider bars featuring dozens of options from around the world. The teaching restaurant Atelier de la Crêpe, which opened in 2018, aligns perfectly with this approach, along with the farm purchased in 2017. This philosophy promotes the integrity of artisan farmers and Breton land and proves that to bring together the world's cultures, it's important to remain faithful to your roots and your terroir.

"TEACHING OTHERS THE PROFESSION ALSO INVOLVES INTRODUCING BRITTANY, ITS CULTURE AND THE QUALITY OF ITS PRODUCTS IN THE EYES OF THE WORLD."

The Crêpier's Craft

Crepes are historically associated with Brittany, but in recent years, people throughout France and abroad have developed a taste for them.

While the profession of crepe maker, or crêpier, has been not well known until now, at Atelier de la Crêpe, crêpiers are considered ambassadors of Breton cultural heritage.

That's the main objective of this school: "Restoring nobility to a simple craft that requires an understanding of movement and precision," says Yves Camdeborde, restaurateur at Comptoir du Relais Saint-Germain and a godfather of the school.

The crêpier's craft involves the mastery of techniques, knowledge of the industry and a solid understanding of artisanal ingredients. Plying this trade is not about being a "crepe seller," as the Larousse dictionary defines it. Just as chefs go through a very demanding training program, the art of the crepe requires crêpiers to become qualified and develop their expertise before they can do it well.

Rooted in a specific geographic area, the crêpier must be committed to sustainability and interact with producers and local artisans. Also, they need to be aware of local food systems and prioritize the local economy. This involves much more than expertise or technical skills; it also calls for knowledge of the iconic products around them.

Because the crêpier's craft has a strong regional base in Brittany, Atelier de la Crêpe's goal is to promote buckwheat and all the other products grown and harvested in the region.

The seasonality of products and local food systems must no longer be an obstacle when it comes to managing a menu but, in fact, be its strength, what makes it different, its main features. This ensures the customer has an authentic, unique and fresh experience every time.

The crêpier is also an intermediary between the various producers and partners, from organic buckwheat and wheat to vegetables to dairy products or the cider that accompanies the tasting of galettes and crepes. The crêpier balances all these products to provide a powerful, quality experience. The crêpier plays a key role between the various producers to select the best products.

The crêpier, like a chef, must be versatile, from management, to cost and stock control, to dining room service. That is why skilled crêpiers are rare and highly sought after in the crepe restaurant market.

While the crêpier's craft evokes traditional techniques and Breton heritage, the challenge of Atelier de la Crêpe is also to modernize a craft that has not been considered one until now. Making crepe restaurants with open kitchens so customers can watch the crêpier's dexterity and precision is a way to showcase the craft.

For those who want to enter this profession, Bertrand Larcher aims to use this international school to kindle or rekindle their desire to do so. The training courses give everyone who loves making crepes and galettes an opportunity to develop their skills to access a growing profession.

"It's actually quite moving to see Bertrand, this guy from Fougères, taking on the buckwheat challenge. This galette bolsters our simple and sincere Breton values. It is a link between humanism and our Breton community. Long live buckwheat. Long live Brittany!" exclaims Éric Beaumard, sommelier and director of the Hotel George V restaurant in Paris and a godfather of the Atelier de la Crêpe school.

NOTE: The quantities and temperatures in this book have been converted from metric and some rounding was done for ease of measuring by volume. When preparing the recipes, please use all metric or all imperial measurements and avoid interchanging the two.

The Atelier de la Crêpe kitchen (left) and the Atelier de la Crêpe training restaurant (right).

CREPES AND GALETTES: STEP BY STEP

1

2

3

4

5

6

MAKES 4 CUPS (1 L), ENOUGH FOR 8 GALETTES

PREPARATION: 10 MINUTES

RESTING TIME: AT LEAST 24 HOURS IN THE FRIDGE AND 30 MINUTES AT ROOM TEMPERATURE

- $2\frac{1}{4}$ cups (320 g) whole-grain (dark) buckwheat flour
- 1 tsp (5 g) fine sea salt
- $2\frac{2}{3}$ cups + $\frac{1}{4}$ cup (710 mL) water, divided

TIP

LETTING THE BATTER REST IMPROVES THE TASTE, TEXTURE AND COLOR OF THE GALETTE.

Galette Batter

1 Combine the flour and salt in a medium bowl.

2 Add $1\frac{1}{3}$ cups (325 mL) water.

3 Mix with your hands to get a smooth batter.

4 Beat the batter with your fingers apart, making upward circular movements to add air. Smooth the top.

5 Pour $\frac{1}{4}$ cup (60 mL) water over the batter to keep it from drying out. Cover the bowl and let rest for at least 24 hours in the fridge or for up to 2 days. Leave the batter at room temperature for 30 minutes before using.

6 Gradually pour the remaining $1\frac{1}{3}$ cups (325 mL) water into the batter, stirring; the batter should not be too liquid. It is now ready to use.

froment

1
2
3
4
5
6

MAKES $3^1/_3$ CUPS (825 ML), ENOUGH FOR 8 CREPES

PREPARATION: 15 MINUTES

- 2 eggs
- $^1/_4$ cup (50 g) granulated sugar
- 2 tsp (10 g) butter
- 2 cups (500 mL) whole milk, divided
- $1^1/_2$ cups (200 g) all-purpose flour

TIP

IF THERE ARE ANY LUMPS, STRAIN THE BATTER USING A FINE-MESH SIEVE.

Crepe Batter

1 Break the eggs into a bowl. Add the sugar.

2 Whisk the eggs with the sugar until the mixture lightens.

3 Melt the butter. Add it to the batter.

4 Add 1 cup (250 mL) of the milk and mix well.

5 Gradually add the flour, whisking until blended.

6 Add the remaining milk. Mix well. It is now ready to be used.

1
2
ATELIER
DE LA CRÊPE
SAINT-MALO
3
4
5
6

COOKING CREPES ON A CREPE MAKER

COOKING CREPES IS DIFFERENT FROM COOKING GALETTES. HERE ARE THE DIFFERENCES:

- FOR STEP 1, BEFORE GREASING THE CREPE MAKER, HEAT TO 430°F (220°C). GREASING LIGHTLY EVERY 3 OR 4 CREPES IS ENOUGH.
- FOR STEP 2, USE A SMALLER LADLE (ABOUT 6 TBSP/90 ML) TO GET THE IDEAL THICKNESS OF CREPE.
- FOR STEP 4, CREPES ARE COOKED AT NO HIGHER THAN 430°F (220°C).
- FOR STEP 5, TO AVOID OVERCOOKING THE CREPE, YOU DON'T NEED TO WAIT FOR THE EDGES TO LIFT; JUST WAIT A FEW SECONDS BEFORE TURNING IT.

EQUIPMENT NEEDED

16-INCH (40 CM) CREPE MAKER
HEATPROOF BRUSH (TO GREASE THE PLATES)
LADLE
CREPE SPREADER
SPATULA

Cooking Galettes on a Crepe Maker

1 Grease the plate of the crepe maker
Greasing is done once the crepe maker is hot: let it heat for a few minutes to 480°F (250°C) for a galette. The preferred fat to use is lard; you can also use grapeseed oil. Brush it over the cast-iron plate using a heatproof brush or greasing tool and spread it uniformly, in a thin layer. When cooking galettes, grease the plate between each galette.

2 Add the batter
To make a galette, use a ladle 3 inches (8 cm) in diameter ($^{1}/_{2}$ cup/125 mL) to pour the batter on the crepe maker (for a 16-inch/40 cm plate). Fill the ladle completely to get a nice galette, adjusting for a smaller size plate if needed. If you are right-handed, hold the ladle in your left hand. The batter is generally poured on the lower left side of the plate (on a clockface, between 6 and 9 o'clock). Once you have poured the batter, you must spread it right away.

3 Spread the batter
Spread the batter using a crepe spreader, called a rozell in Breton. Once the batter is on the plate, spread it clockwise as you make repeated semicircle motions. Be sure to gather all the galette batter with the spreader with each movement. Hold the spreader between your thumb and index finger, keeping it almost parallel to the plate. Hold it lightly, without applying any pressure.

4 Cook the galette
For galettes, the cooking temperature should be between 480°F and 525°F (250°C and 270°C). The cooking time for galettes is longer than the cooking time for crepes. Cook until the edges of the galette start to lift from the plate. To make a filled galette, add the filling as directed in the recipes.

5 Flip the galette
To serve a plain galette, or to fill it on the plate, the galette can be flipped. To do this, peel off the whole galette using a stainless-steel spatula and turn it over to cook it quickly on the second side (about 30 seconds).

6 Serve or fill the galette
Once the second side is cooked, you can use your spatula to serve the galette on a plate.

ATELIER
DE LA CRÊPE
SAINT-MALO

1

ATELIER
DE LA CRÊPE
SAINT-MALO

2

3

4

COOKING GALETTES IN A SKILLET

COOKING GALETTES IS DIFFERENT FROM COOKING CREPES. HERE ARE THE DIFFERENCES:

- FOR STEP 2, USE A LARGER LADLE (ABOUT $1/2$ CUP/125 ML) TO GET THE IDEAL THICKNESS OF GALETTE, DEPENDING ON SIZE OF SKILLET.
- FOR STEP 3, FOR THE COOKING TIME OF THE FIRST SIDE OF THE GALETTE, WATCH THE EDGES. WHEN THEY LIFT FROM THE PAN, THE GALETTE IS READY TO BE FILLED, OR FLIPPED TO COOK THE SECOND SIDE TO SERVE PLAIN OR TO FILL ON THE SERVING PLATE.

EQUIPMENT NEEDED

SKILLET
LADLE
SPATULA

TIP

IF YOU WANT TO FILL A GALETTE, BRUSH IT WITH MELTED BUTTER AND PLACE THE INGREDIENTS ON IT RIGHT AFTER YOU HAVE SPREAD THE BATTER WITHOUT FLIPPING, AS DIRECTED IN THE RECIPES.

Cooking Crepes in a Skillet

1 Prepare your equipment
To cook crepes, choose a 10-inch (25 cm) skillet with a nonstick surface, a flat base and low sides to make it easier to turn the crepe. Heat the skillet over medium-high heat until very hot. To grease the skillet, use an oil that can tolerate high heat well and has a neutral taste, such as grapeseed oil. Spread a fine layer of oil on the skillet using a paper towel to avoid having too much fat.

2 Add and spread the batter
Using a ladle (about 6 tbsp/90 mL), pour the batter on the skillet and immediately spread the batter by making a circular motion with your wrist to tilt the pan so you get a thin crepe. Use less batter if your pan is smaller. If the batter does not adhere to the skillet, too much oil was used. The batter needs to spread evenly over the entire surface of the skillet for uniform cooking.

3 Cook the crepe
As with cooking on a crepe maker, the crepe will be cooked on both sides. The crepe must adhere to the surface. If the temperature is too low, the crepe will be very pale. The first crepe allows you to check that the cooking temperature is correct.

4 Turn over the crepe
For this step, you can flip the crepe or turn it over more gently using a spatula (use one that won't scratch the skillet's non-stick coating). To flip it, start by making sure the crepe is not sticking to the skillet. Next, hold the skillet by the handle with both hands, then tilt it away from you and give a flick of the wrist upward to flip the crepe onto the other side. This may take a little practice. Cook the second side for about 1 minute, just until dry looking.

Folding

Folding is an important step in the presentation of galettes and crepes. Folding must always be done with a spatula (except for rolled and beggar's purse folds). For crepes and galettes to take center stage on the plate, they must be folded geometrically and adjusted to the size of the plate on which they will be served. Although there are no official rules for folding, the choice of fold is considered by crepe makers to showcase a product, filling or garnish. Only classic crepes use a common fold that we can find in many creperies, such as the full fold or fan-shaped fold.

Quarters

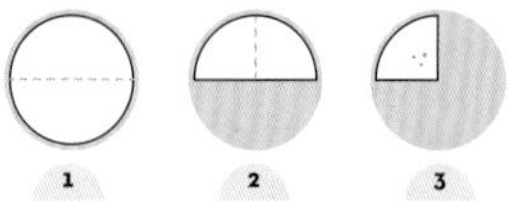

This fold is one of the easiest to do and is adapted for small plates. Start by folding the crepe in half, then fold it again in the middle by folding the right side over the left side.

Quarters (variation)

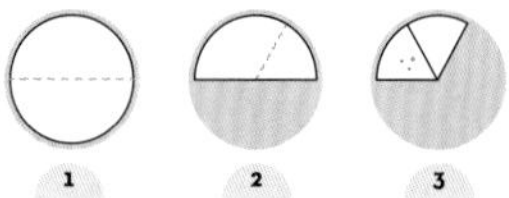

A variation of the quarters fold involves partially folding the right side over the left side, as shown.

Open square (full fold)

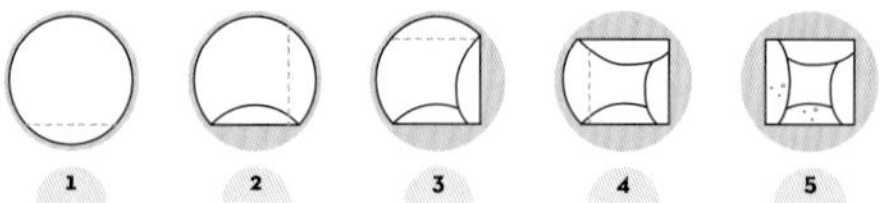

This fold is used often in crepe restaurants. It allows you to showcase the filling, such as a fried egg. Fold up the lower side around $1\frac{1}{2}$ times the width of the spatula and repeat on the other 3 sides.

Closed square

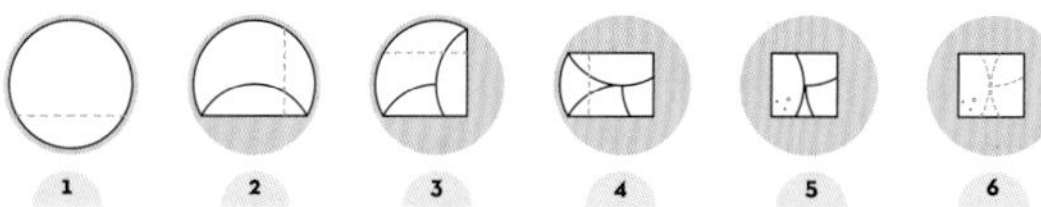

The closed square is done the same way as the open square. But instead, 4 sides of the crepe are folded in enough to completely cover the filling. The filled crepe is turned over and served on the plate with the folded side down.

Closed rectangle

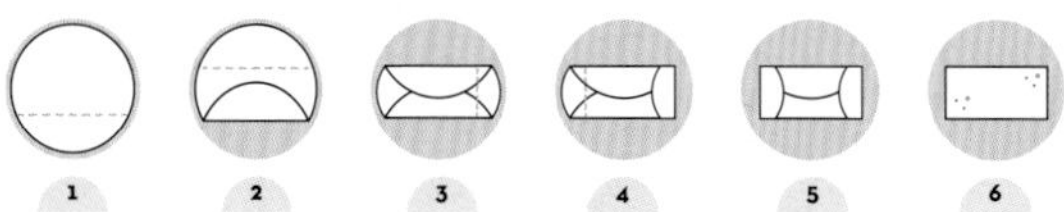

The closed rectangle is a variation of the closed square. For steps 2 and 3, the sides must be folded up more than for the closed square. On the other hand, for steps 4 and 5, the sides must be folded up more narrowly. The filled crepe is turned over and served with the folded side down.

* *We have used the generic term "crepe" in the instructions, but all the folds apply to both crepes and galettes.*

Rolled

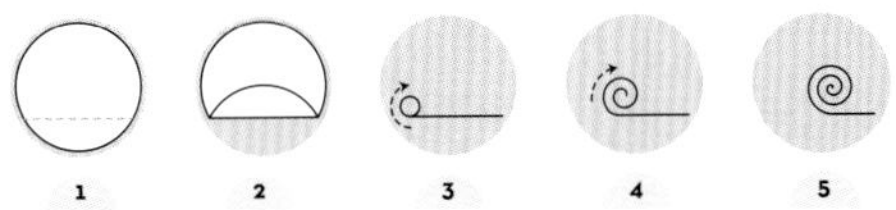

To be able to roll the crepe properly, you must let it cool after cooking. Once the filling is spread over the whole surface, use both hands to tightly roll the entire width of the crepe. Once the crepe is rolled, wrap it tightly in plastic wrap and refrigerate. Then you can cut it into bite-size pieces.

Open triangle

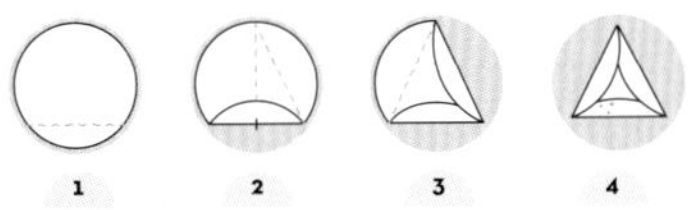

The open triangle is less common and takes practice. The filling is placed on the crepe before folding to make folding into a triangle easier. Start by folding up the lower part of the crepe over about one-third of its width, then fold in the right side, from the lower right corner to the center of the top of the crepe. Repeat this process to fold the left side. The filling is visible in the middle.

Closed triangle

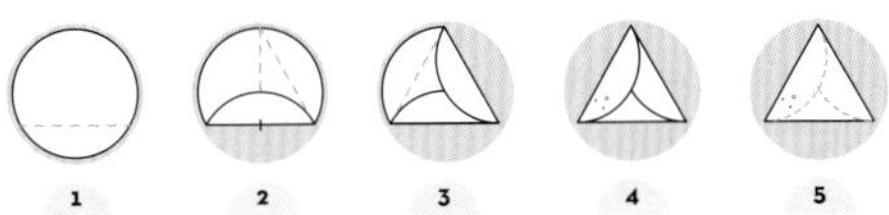

The closed triangle is the one most often used when fillings are a topping on the crepe. You must fold the edges a little wider than for the open triangle so they meet once they are folded. Next, you need to turn over the crepe and place it on the serving plate, then add any topping.

Fan

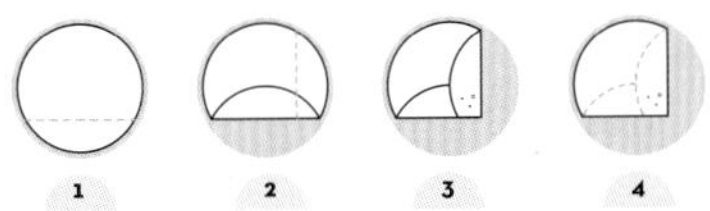

The fan is usually used for the butter and brown sugar crepe and other classic recipes. Start by folding the lower part of the crepe over about one-third of its width (adjust the width to the size of the plate). At a right angle, fold the right side over the same width to get a symmetrical fan fold. The crepe can be served on the plate right side up or upside down.

Octagon

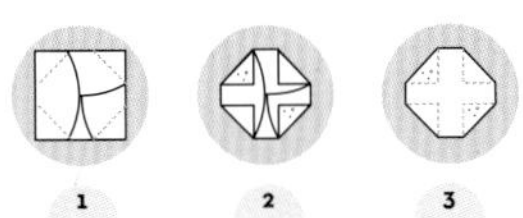

This fold is done in 6 steps. The first steps involve making a closed square, but leave the folded side up. Then fold in the 4 corners toward the center of the crepe without having them touch. The filled crepe is then turned over and served with the folded side down.

Beggar's purse

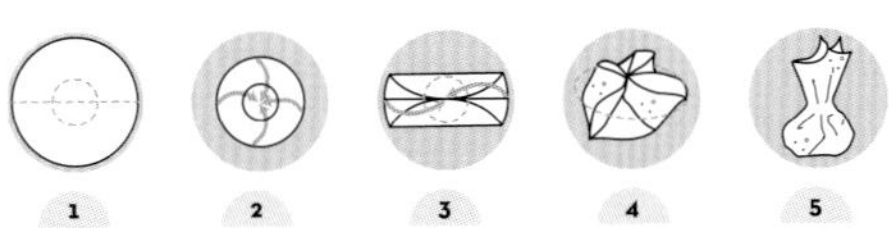

The beggar's purse is suited to filled crepes, allowing for more volume. Place the crepe on the serving plate. Place the filling in the center of the crepe, then close up the crepe by folding in the sides two at a time toward the center above the filling. The purse can be held closed with a toothpick or some edible string, for example.

The kitchens of Atelier de la Crêpe (left) and the training restaurant of Atelier de la Crêpe (right)

THE CLASSIC RECIPES

Butter Galette with Salad

(The Classic)

MAKES 4 GALETTES
PREPARATION: 10 MINUTES
COOKING TIME: 8 MINUTES

FOR THE CIDER VINAIGRETTE

- 2 tbsp + 2 tsp (40 g) Dijon mustard
- $1\frac{1}{2}$ tsp (8 g) fine salt
- 2 tsp (4 g) ground white pepper
- 1 cup (250 mL) sunflower oil
- $\frac{2}{3}$ cup (150 mL) olive oil
- $\frac{1}{3}$ cup (75 mL) apple cider vinegar

FOR THE GALETTES

- $\frac{1}{4}$ cup (60 g) butter, divided
- 2 cups (500 mL) galette batter (see recipe on page 15)

FOR THE SALAD

- $4\frac{1}{2}$ cups (160 g) salad greens

TIP

ADD A BIT OF BUTTER ON THE GALETTE JUST BEFORE SERVING.

HOW TO FOLD

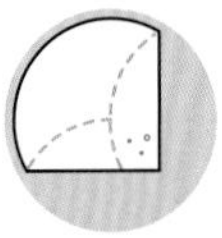

Start by making the vinaigrette: Combine the mustard, salt and pepper in a bowl. Using a whisk, mix these ingredients while drizzling in the two oils. Add the vinegar and whisk again.

For the galettes: Melt 2 tbsp (30 g) of the butter. Cut the remaining butter into small pieces. Heat the crepe maker to 480°F (250°C) (or the skillet) and grease as directed. Pour and spread $\frac{1}{2}$ cup (125 mL) of the batter evenly. Brush the galette with some of the melted butter. When the edges start to lift, use the spatula to fold the galette into a fan shape. Turn over the galette using the spatula. Place small pieces of butter on the surface of the galette and, when they start to melt, remove the galette from the crepe maker (or skillet) and place it folded side down on a plate.

Place the salad greens in a salad bowl. Dress with the vinaigrette to taste and serve one-quarter of the salad alongside the galette.

Repeat the above steps for the other 3 galettes.

Refrigerate any extra vinaigrette in a jar for up 2 months.

MAKES 4 GALETTES

PREPARATION: 7 MINUTES

COOKING TIME: 8 MINUTES

- 2 cups (500 mL) galette batter (see recipe on page 15)
- 3 tbsp (40 g) butter, melted
- 4 eggs
- 1 cup + 6 tbsp (160 g) grated Emmental cheese
- $5\frac{1}{2}$ oz (165 g) deli smoked ham, sliced

TIP

SPREAD THE EGG WHITE OVER THE WHOLE GALETTE WITH THE SPATULA, HOLDING THE YOLK IN THE CENTER WITH YOUR HAND.

THIS RECIPE CONTAINS RAW OR UNDERCOOKED EGGS. IF YOU ARE CONCERNED ABOUT THE FOOD SAFETY OF RAW EGGS, SUBSTITUTE PASTEURIZED EGGS IN THE SHELL.

HOW TO FOLD

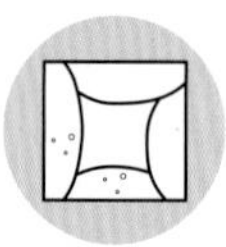

Galette Complète

Heat the crepe maker to 480°F (250°C) (or the skillet) and grease as directed. Pour and spread $\frac{1}{2}$ cup (125 mL) of the batter evenly. Brush the galette with some of the melted butter. Break 1 egg in the center of the galette and spread the egg white with the spatula. Sprinkle with one-quarter of the Emmental, add one-quarter of the ham and cook. When the edges start to lift, use the spatula to fold the galette into an open square (full fold). Brush the folded edges of the galette with melted butter.

Remove the galette from the crepe maker (or skillet) and serve it on a plate.

Repeat the above steps for the other 3 galettes.

Galette Complète

with Creamed Mushrooms

MAKES 4 GALETTES
PREPARATION: 30 MINUTES
COOKING TIME: 15 MINUTES

FOR THE CREAMED MUSHROOMS

- 8 oz (250 g) button mushrooms
- 2 tsp (10 g) butter
- $\frac{1}{2}$ tsp (2 g) fine salt
- $\frac{1}{4}$ cup (60 mL) heavy or whipping (35%) cream
- Pepper

FOR THE GALETTES

- 2 cups (500 mL) galette batter (see recipe on page 15)
- 3 tbsp (40 g) butter, melted
- 4 eggs
- 1 cup + 6 tbsp (160 g) grated Emmental cheese
- $5\frac{1}{2}$ oz (165 g) deli smoked ham, sliced

Prepare the creamed mushrooms: Cut the mushrooms into $\frac{1}{8}$-inch (3 mm) thick slices. In a skillet, melt the butter over high heat, then add the mushrooms and salt. Cook until the liquid released by the mushrooms evaporates. Add the cream and cook until thickened. Add pepper to taste.

Heat the crepe maker to 480°F (250°C) (or the skillet) and grease as directed. Pour and spread $\frac{1}{2}$ cup (125 mL) of the batter evenly. Brush the galette with some of the melted butter. Break 1 egg in the center and spread the egg white with the spatula. Sprinkle with one-quarter of the Emmental and add one-quarter of the ham. Add one-quarter of the creamed mushrooms and cook. When the edges start to lift, use the spatula to fold the galette into an open triangle. Brush the folded edges of the galette with melted butter.

Remove the galette from the crepe maker (or skillet) and serve it on a plate.

Repeat the above steps for the other 3 galettes.

TIPS

BEFORE ADDING THE CREAM, MAKE SURE THE LIQUID FROM THE MUSHROOMS HAS REDUCED.

THIS RECIPE CONTAINS RAW OR UNDERCOOKED EGGS. IF YOU ARE CONCERNED ABOUT THE FOOD SAFETY OF RAW EGGS, SUBSTITUTE PASTEURIZED EGGS IN THE SHELL.

HOW TO FOLD

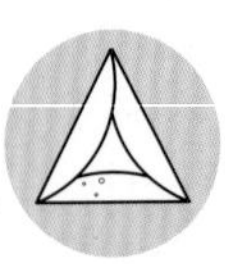

Galette Complète

with Onion Chutney

MAKES 4 GALETTES
Preparation: 30 minutes
Cooking time: 12 minutes

FOR THE ONION CHUTNEY

- 1 lb (500 g) yellow onions
- 2 tbsp (30 mL) olive oil
- ½ tsp (2 g) fine salt
- 2 tsp (10 mL) balsamic vinegar
- 2 tbsp (25 g) granulated sugar

FOR THE GALETTES

- 2 cups (500 mL) galette batter (see recipe on page 15)
- 3 tbsp (40 g) butter, melted
- 4 eggs
- 1 cup + 6 tbsp (160 g) grated Emmental cheese
- 5½ oz (165 g) deli smoked ham, sliced

HOW TO FOLD

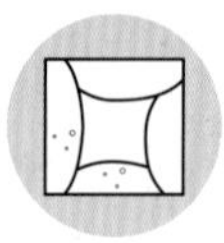

Make the onion chutney: Peel the onions and cut them into thin slices. In a skillet, heat the olive oil over medium heat. Add the sliced onions and salt. Sauté for a few minutes, then add the vinegar and sugar and turn the heat to high. Cook until the liquid has evaporated. Set aside.

Heat the crepe maker to 480°F (250°C) (or the skillet) and grease as directed. Pour and spread ½ cup (125 mL) of the batter evenly. Brush the galette with some of the melted butter. Break 1 egg in the center and spread the egg white with the spatula. Sprinkle one-quarter of the Emmental on top. Add one-quarter of the ham. Add the chutney to taste and cook. When the edges start to lift, use the spatula to fold the galette into an open square (full fold). Brush the folded edges of the galette with melted butter.

Remove the galette from the crepe maker (or skillet) and serve it on a plate.

Repeat the above steps for the other 3 galettes.

Freeze any extra chutney in an airtight container for up to 2 months.

MAKES 4 CREPES
PREPARATION: 2 MINUTES
COOKING TIME: 10 MINUTES

- $1^{2}/_{3}$ cups (400 mL) crepe batter (see recipe on page 17)
- 3 tbsp (40 g) butter, melted
- 3 tbsp (40 g) packed brown sugar

HOW TO FOLD

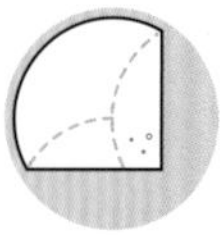

Butter and Brown Sugar Crepe

Heat the crepe maker to 430°F (220°C) (or the skillet) and grease as directed. Pour and spread one-quarter (about $6^{1}/_{2}$ tbsp/100 mL) of the batter evenly. Cook both sides as directed. Brush the crepe with some of the melted butter.

Use the spatula to fold the crepe into a fan shape, then place it folded side down on a serving plate.

Brush the crepe with melted butter and sprinkle with one-quarter of the brown sugar.

Repeat the above steps for the other 3 crepes.

ATELIER

Salted Caramel Crepe

MAKES 4 CREPES
PREPARATION: 5 MINUTES
COOKING TIME: 15 MINUTES

FOR THE SALTED CARAMEL

- $\frac{1}{4}$ cup (60 mL) heavy or whipping (35%) cream
- 3 tbsp + 1 tsp (50 g) salted butter
- 4 tsp (20 mL) water
- 6 tbsp (80 g) granulated sugar

FOR THE CREPES

- $1\frac{2}{3}$ cups (400 mL) crepe batter (see recipe on page 17)
- 3 tbsp (40 g) butter, melted

TIP

TO MAKE THE CARAMEL, ADD THE CREAM GRADUALLY, WHISKING VIGOROUSLY SO IT DOESN'T BURN.

HOW TO FOLD

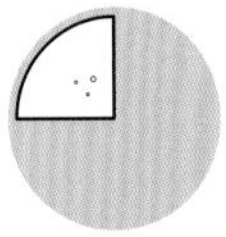

Make the salted caramel: Warm the cream in a saucepan over low heat. In another saucepan, melt the butter. Add the water and sugar to the butter, stirring well. Over high heat, cook until you get a soft caramel. Stir and watch for splatters. Remove the pan from the heat. Add the warm cream and mix well.

Heat the crepe maker to 430°F (220°C) (or the skillet) and grease as directed. Pour and spread one-quarter (about $6\frac{1}{2}$ tbsp/100 mL) of the batter evenly. Cook both sides as directed. Brush the crepe with some of the melted butter. Use the spatula to fold the crepe into quarters, then place it on a serving plate and pour one-quarter of the caramel over it.

Repeat the above steps for the other 3 crepes.

Crepe with Flambéed Grand Marnier

MAKES 4 CREPES
PREPARATION: 5 MINUTES
COOKING TIME: 15 MINUTES

- $1\frac{2}{3}$ cups (400 mL) crepe batter (see recipe page 17)
- 3 tbsp (40 g) butter, melted
- $\frac{1}{3}$ cup (75 mL) Grand Marnier

TIP

MAKE SURE THE GRAND MARNIER IS HOT ENOUGH TO FLAMBÉ.

HOW TO FOLD

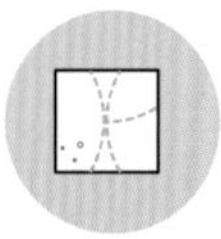

Heat the crepe maker to 430°F (220°C) (or the skillet) and grease as directed. Pour and spread one-quarter (about $6\frac{1}{2}$ tbsp/100 mL) of the batter evenly. Cook both sides as directed. Brush the crepe with some of the melted butter. Use the spatula to fold the crepe in a closed square. Place it on a serving plate and drizzle with melted butter.

Repeat the above steps for the other 3 crepes.

Heat the Grand Marnier in a small saucepan, flambé using a gas lighter, and quickly pour it over the crepes.

MAKES 4 CREPES

PREPARATION: 5 MINUTES

COOKING TIME: 10 MINUTES

- $1\frac{2}{3}$ cups (400 mL) crepe batter (see recipe on page 17)
- 3 tbsp (40 g) butter, melted
- $\frac{3}{4}$ cup (120 g) small chocolate pieces of your choice

TIP

SERVE ON A HEATED PLATE SO THE CHOCOLATE MELTS.

HOW TO FOLD

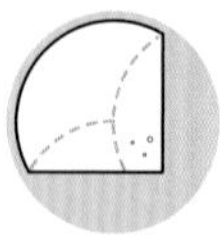

Crepe with Chocolate

Heat the crepe maker to 430°F (220°C) (or the skillet) and grease as directed. Pour and spread one-quarter (about $6\frac{1}{2}$ tbsp/100 mL) of the batter evenly. Cook both sides as directed. Brush the crepe with some of the melted butter. Use the spatula to fold the crepe in a fan shape, then place it fold side down on a plate.

Brush the crepe with melted butter and sprinkle with one-quarter of the chocolate pieces.

Repeat the above steps for the other 3 crepes.

Atelier de la Crêpe is an international school specializing in teaching the trade of crêpier (crepe maker) to professionals and individuals. It's a place for sharing ideas, enjoying good food and passing on knowledge where we express our commitment to Breton heritage.

As part of its educational approach, Atelier de la Crêpe has a training restaurant where interns learn production and service techniques and make galettes and crepes using local products with their instructors.

farine
DE BLÉ

Port of Saint-Malo (left) and Terre Nueve quay (right)

SPRING RECIPES

MAKES 4 GALETTES

PREPARATION: 30 MINUTES

COOKING TIME: 20 MINUTES

FOR THE VEGETABLES

- 12 green asparagus spears
- 4 handfuls green peas
- Salt

FOR THE CHORIZO SAUCE

- 1 shallot
- 1 tsp (5 g) butter
- 4 tsp (20 mL) cider
- 2 tbsp (20 g) finely diced cured chorizo sausage
- $\frac{1}{4}$ cup (60 mL) heavy or whipping (35%) cream

FOR THE GALETTES

- 2 cups (500 mL) galette batter (see recipe on page 15)
- 3 tbsp (40 g) butter, melted
- 1 cup (120 g) grated Emmental cheese

TIP

WHEN THE PEAS ARE BLANCHED, POUR COLD WATER GRADUALLY INTO THE BOILING WATER TO KEEP THEIR SKINS SMOOTH.

HOW TO FOLD

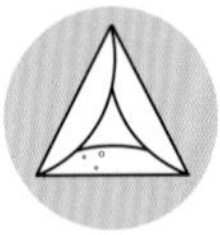

Galette with Green Asparagus, Peas and Chorizo Sauce

Prepare the vegetables: Blanch the asparagus in boiling water in a saucepan, then run under cold water. Drain and cut the spears into segments. Shell the peas, if necessary, and blanch the peas in boiling salted water in a saucepan, then drain. Set aside.

Make the sauce: Peel and chop the shallot. Melt the butter in a saucepan on high heat and sauté the shallot until softened. Add the cider and bring to a boil. Add the chorizo and sauté until lightly browned. Add the cream. Set aside.

Heat the crepe maker to 480°F (250°C) (or the skillet) and grease as directed. Pour and spread $\frac{1}{2}$ cup (125 mL) of the batter evenly. Brush the galette with some of the melted butter and sprinkle with one-quarter of the Emmental. Add one-quarter of the vegetables and one-quarter of the sauce, then cook. When the edges start to lift, use the spatula to fold the galette into an open triangle. Brush the folded edges of the galette with melted butter.

Remove the galette from the crepe maker (or skillet) and serve on a plate.

Repeat the above steps for the other 3 crepes.

MAKES 4 GALETTES
PREPARATION: 35 MINUTES
COOKING TIME: 20 MINUTES

White Asparagus and Fried Egg Galette

with Emmental and Blue Cheese Sauce

FOR THE BLUE CHEESE SAUCE

- 1 shallot
- 1 tsp (5 g) butter
- $\frac{1}{4}$ cup (60 mL) heavy or whipping (35%) cream
- $1\frac{2}{3}$ oz (50 g) French blue cheese, such as Bleu d'Auvergne
- Sugar

FOR THE GALETTES

- Salt
- Sugar
- 4 white asparagus spears
- 2 cups (500 mL) galette batter (see recipe on page 15)
- 4 eggs
- 1 cup (120 g) grated Emmental cheese
- 2 tsp (10 g) butter

HOW TO FOLD

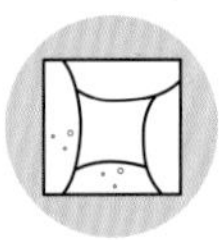

Make the sauce: Peel and chop the shallot. Melt the butter in a saucepan on high heat, then add the shallot and sauté over low heat. Add the cream and chunks of blue cheese. Add a pinch of sugar and cook until golden.

Prepare the asparagus: Prepare an ice bath. Heat 2 cups (500 mL) water in a saucepan with a pinch of salt and sugar. Peel the asparagus. Place the asparagus spears in the boiling water and cook for 5 minutes. Remove the asparagus from the boiling water and plunge them into the ice bath. Cut each spear into 4 segments on the diagonal.

Heat the crepe maker to 480°F (250°C) (or the skillet) and grease as directed. Pour and spread $\frac{1}{2}$ cup (125 mL) of the batter evenly. Brush the galette with some of the melted butter. Break 1 egg in the center and spread the egg white with the spatula. Sprinkle one-quarter of the Emmental around the yolk. Add 4 asparagus segments, pour one-quarter of the blue cheese sauce over the top and cook. When the edges start to lift, use the spatula to fold the galette into an open square (full fold). Brush the folded edges of the galette with melted butter.

Remove the galette from the crepe maker (or skillet) and serve it on a plate.

Repeat the above steps for the other 3 crepes.

Galette with Surimi and Vegetables

in Béchamel Sauce

MAKES 4 GALETTES
Preparation: 20 MINUTES
Cooking time: 20 MINUTES

FOR THE VEGETABLES

- 1⅔ cups (150 g) sliced leeks (white and light green parts only)
- 1 cup (115 g) cauliflower florets

FOR THE BÉCHAMEL SAUCE

- 3 tbsp (40 g) butter
- ⅓ cup (45 g) all-purpose flour
- 1⅔ cups (400 mL) milk
- 2 pinches of salt

FOR THE GALETTES

- 2 cups (500 mL) galette batter (see recipe on page 15)
- 3 tbsp (40 g) butter, melted
- 4 oz (125 g) surimi, pulled into strands
- 4 pinches of ground Espelette chile pepper

TIP

SURIMI IS A SEAFOOD PASTE SHAPED TO MIMIC THE TEXTURE AND LOOK OF CRAB OR LOBSTER. IT'S FOUND IN THE SEAFOOD SECTION AT GROCERY STORES.

HOW TO FOLD

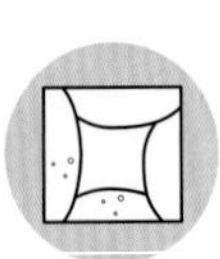

Prepare the vegetables: Cook the leeks in boiling salted water until tender. Remove the leeks with a slotted spoon and squeeze to remove all the water. Blanch the cauliflower florets in the boiling salted water. They should be a little crunchy. Drain.

Make the béchamel sauce: In a saucepan over high heat, melt the butter, add the flour all at once and whisk. Slowly add the milk, stirring well to avoid lumps. Cook, whisking, until thickened; add the salt. Stir the vegetables into the béchamel sauce.

Heat the crepe maker to 480°F (250°C) (or the skillet) and grease as directed. Pour and spread ½ cup (125 mL) of the batter evenly. Brush the galette with some of the melted butter. Place one-quarter of the vegetables in béchamel in the center of the galette and add one-quarter of the surimi, then cook. When the edges start to lift, use the spatula to fold the galette into an open square (full fold). Brush the folded edges of the galette with melted butter. Sprinkle with a pinch of chile pepper.

Remove the galette from the crepe maker (or skillet) and serve it on a plate.

Repeat the above steps for the other 3 crepes.

MAKES 4 GALETTES
PREPARATION: 20 MINUTES
COOKING TIME: 30 MINUTES

FOR THE MASHED POTATOES WITH SEAWEED TARTARE

- 1 lb (500 g) potatoes
- $1\frac{1}{2}$ tsp (20 g) butter, melted
- $2\frac{1}{2}$ tbsp (37 mL) olive oil
- $\frac{1}{4}$ cup (65 g) seaweed tartare

FOR THE GALETTES

- 2 cups (500 mL) galette batter (see recipe on page 15)
- 4 tsp (20 g) seaweed tartare

TIP

AVOID USING A MIXER OR BLENDER FOR THE POTATOES. OPT FOR MASHED RATHER THAN PURÉED.

HOW TO FOLD

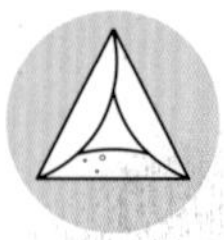

Mashed Potato and Seaweed Tartare Galette

Make the mashed potatoes: Peel the potatoes and cut them into large chunks. Place the potatoes in boiling salted water in a saucepan and cook for 20 minutes. Drain and place them in a large bowl. Mash the potatoes with a fork or potato masher, leaving some chunks. Add the melted butter and olive oil and mix well. Let cool, then add the seaweed tartare.

Heat the crepe maker to 480°F (250°C) (or the skillet) and grease as directed. Pour and spread $\frac{1}{2}$ cup (125 mL) of the batter evenly. Brush the galette with some of the melted butter. Add one-quarter of the mashed potatoes to the center of the galette, then cook. When the edges start to lift, use the spatula to fold the galette into an open triangle. Brush the folded edges of the galette with melted butter. Add 1 tsp (5 mL) seaweed tartare.

Remove the galette from the crepe maker (or skillet) and place it on a serving plate.

Repeat the above steps for the other 3 galettes.

Rolled Salmon Mousse and Dill Galette

MAKES 1 ROLL

PREPARATION: 15 MINUTES
COOKING TIME: 5 MINUTES
RESTING TIME: 30 MINUTES IN THE FRIDGE

FOR THE FILLING

- $\frac{1}{4}$ cup (60 mL) heavy or whipping (35%) cream
- 1$\frac{3}{4}$ oz (50 g) smoked salmon, chopped
- 1 tbsp (3 g) chopped fresh dill

FOR THE GALETTES

- $\frac{1}{2}$ cup (125 mL) galette batter (see recipe on page 15)
- 1 tsp (5 g) butter, melted

TIP

CHILL THE GALETTE BEFORE SLICING IT INTO BITE-SIZE PIECES.

HOW TO FOLD

Make the filling: Whip the cream. Fold in the salmon. Sprinkle with chopped dill.

Heat the crepe maker to 480°F (250°C) (or the skillet) and grease as directed. Pour and spread the batter evenly. Brush the galette with melted butter, then cook. When the edges start to lift, flip it over and cook the second side as directed. With the spatula, place the galette on a cutting board. Let cool.

Place the salmon mixture along the full width of the galette and roll up tightly.

Place the roll in plastic wrap in the fridge for 30 minutes so the salmon mousse sets.

Cut the roll into bite-size pieces and arrange on a plate.

Galette with Smoked Herring, Sautéed Fennel, Potatoes and Creamed Dill

MAKES 4 GALETTES

PREPARATION: 30 MINUTES

COOKING TIME: 20 MINUTES

FOR THE VEGETABLES

- 1 cup + 2 tbsp (100 g) finely chopped fennel bulb
- 4 tsp (20 g) melted butter
- 7 oz (210 g) potato (about 1 medium)

FOR THE CREAMED DILL

- $\frac{3}{4}$ cup (175 mL) thick crème fraîche
- 7 tbsp (20 g) chopped fresh dill

FOR THE GALETTES

- 2 cups (500 mL) galette batter (see recipe on page 15)
- 2 tsp (10 g) butter, melted
- $1\frac{1}{2}$ oz (45 g) smoked herring fillets

TIPS

MAKE SURE THE FENNEL IS NICE AND CRISP.

RESERVE ANY EXTRA CREAMED DILL IN THE REFRIGERATOR FOR UP TO 3 DAYS.

HOW TO FOLD

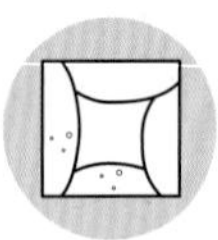

Prepare the vegetables: In a skillet, sauté the fennel in butter until slightly wilted but still crunchy. Set aside.

Meanwhile, cook the potato for 15 minutes in boiling salted water, then drain. Peel and cut the potato into $\frac{1}{2}$-inch (1 cm) slices. Set aside.

Prepare the creamed dill: In a bowl, whisk together the crème fraîche and chopped dill.

Heat the crepe maker to 480°F (250°C) (or the skillet) and grease as directed. Pour and spread $\frac{1}{2}$ cup (125 mL) of the batter evenly. Brush the galette with some of the melted butter. Place one-quarter of the potato in the center, then add one-quarter of the smoked herring and one-quarter of the sautéed fennel. Add 3 tbsp (45 mL) creamed dill and cook. When the edges start to lift, use the spatula to fold the galette into an open square (full fold). Brush the folded edges of the galette with melted butter.

Remove the galette from the crepe maker (or skillet) and serve it on a plate.

Repeat the above steps for the other 3 galettes.

MAKES 4 CREPES

PREPARATION: 30 MINUTES

COOKING TIME: 6 HOURS FOR THE MERINGUE, 10 MINUTES FOR THE CURD, 8 MINUTES FOR THE CREPES

FOR THE MERINGUE

- 2 tbsp (30 g) egg white (about 1 egg)
- 3 tbsp (25 g) confectioners' (icing) sugar
- 2 tbsp (25 g) superfine granulated sugar

FOR THE LEMON CURD

- 2 eggs
- $\frac{1}{4}$ cup (50 g) superfine granulated sugar
- $\frac{1}{4}$ cup (60 mL) lemon juice
- $\frac{1}{4}$ cup (60 g) butter, cut into small pieces

FOR THE CREPES

- $1\frac{2}{3}$ cups (400 mL) crepe batter (see recipe on page 17)
- 3 tbsp (40 g) butter, melted

TIP

WHEN COOKING THE CURD, THE TEMPERATURE OF THE WATER SHOULD NOT BE TOO HOT TO AVOID SCRAMBLING THE EGGS MIXTURE.

HOW TO FOLD

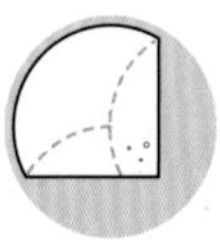

Lemon Meringue Crepe

Make the meringue: Preheat the oven to 200°F (95°C). Using an electric mixer, manual beaters or a whisk, beat the egg white while gradually adding the confectioners' sugar and granulated sugar. Using a pastry bag or a tablespoon, place the mixture in small mounds on a baking sheet lined with parchment paper. Bake for about 6 hours, until the meringue is crispy. Let cool.

Make the lemon curd: Whisk the eggs with the sugar in a heatproof bowl until the mixture lightens in color. Place the mixture over a saucepan of simmering water and add the lemon juice. Cook, whisking, until the curd is thickened. Add the butter and stir until melted and the texture is creamy. Set aside.

Heat the crepe maker to 430°F (220°C) (or the skillet) and grease as directed. Pour and spread one-quarter (about $6\frac{1}{2}$ tbsp/100 mL) of the batter evenly. Brush the crepe with some of the melted butter. Use the spatula to fold the crepe into a fan shape.

Remove the crepe from the crepe maker (or skillet) and serve it on a plate.

Spoon one-quarter of the lemon curd on the crepe, then garnish with crumbled meringues.

Repeat the above steps for the other 3 crepes.

MAKES 4 CREPES
PREPARATION: 30 MINUTES
COOKING TIME: 18 MINUTES
RESTING TIME: 1 NIGHT IN THE FRIDGE

POACHED APRICOT CREPE

WITH HONEY, LEMON AND TOASTED ALMONDS

FOR THE POACHED APRICOTS

- 6 apricots
- 2 cups (500 mL) water
- $\frac{3}{4}$ cup (150 g) granulated sugar
- 4 tsp (20 mL) lemon juice

FOR THE HONEY-LEMON MIXTURE

- Half lemon, about $1\frac{3}{4}$ oz (50 g)
- 5 tbsp (100 g) honey

FOR THE CREPES

- $\frac{2}{3}$ cup (60 g) toasted sliced almonds
- $1\frac{2}{3}$ cups (400 mL) crepe batter (see recipe on page 17)
- 3 tbsp (40 g) butter, melted
- Vanilla ice cream, optional

The day before, prepare the apricots: Peel the apricots, cut them in half and remove the pits. Combine the water, sugar and lemon juice in a large saucepan. Bring to a boil, then add the fruit. Turn off the heat, cover the pan and let the apricots soak in the syrup overnight at room temperature.

The day of serving, make the honey-lemon mixture: Squeeze the lemon and mix the honey with the juice. Set aside.

Preheat the oven to 350°F (180°C). Place the almonds on a baking sheet and toast until golden.

Heat the crepe maker to 430°F (220°C) (or the skillet) and grease as directed. Pour and spread one-quarter (about $6\frac{1}{2}$ tbsp/100 mL) of the batter evenly. Cook, flipping, as directed. Brush the crepe with some of the melted butter. Use a spatula to fold the crepe into a triangle, then place it folded side down on a plate.

Repeat the above steps for the other 3 crepes.

Brush the crepes with melted butter, then top each with 3 poached apricot halves, one-quarter of the honey-lemon mixture and one-quarter of the toasted almonds. Add a scoop of vanilla ice cream, if desired.

TIP

IF THE APRICOTS AREN'T FULLY RIPE, COOK THEM A LITTLE.

IF THE APRICOTS ARE VERY RIPE, SIMPLY ADD THEM TO THE HOT SYRUP WITHOUT COOKING THEM.

HOW TO FOLD

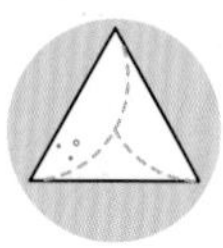

MAKES 4 CREPES

PREPARATION: 30 MINUTES

COOKING TIME: 8 MINUTES

RESTING TIME: 1 NIGHT IN THE FRIDGE

FOR THE CHERRY PRESERVES

- $2\frac{1}{4}$ cups (300 g) cherries
- $1\frac{1}{4}$ cups (300 mL) kirsch
- $\frac{2}{3}$ cup (150 mL) white wine
- 5 tbsp (60 g) superfine granulated sugar
- $\frac{1}{3}$ cup (80 mL) lemon juice

FOR THE WHIPPED CREAM

- $\frac{1}{2}$ cup (125 mL) heavy or whipping (35%) cream
- 1 tbsp (8 g) confectioners' (icing) sugar

FOR THE CREPES

- $1\frac{2}{3}$ cups (400 mL) crepe batter (see recipe on page 17)
- 3 tbsp (40 g) butter, melted

TIPS

TO GET A NICE QUENELLE OF WHIPPED CREAM, PLACE YOUR UTENSILS IN THE FRIDGE BEFOREHAND TO CHILL.

RESERVE ANY EXTRA CHERRY PRESERVES IN A JAR IN THE FRIDGE FOR UP TO 1 MONTH.

HOW TO FOLD

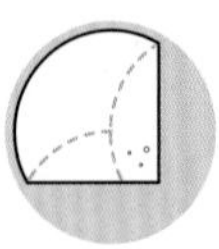

CREPE WITH CHERRY PRESERVES

AND WHIPPED CREAM

The day before, prepare the cherry preserves: Pit the cherries. In a saucepan, combine the kirsch and white wine, then heat on low. Add the sugar and lemon juice. Add the cherries and cook for about 8 minutes. Turn off the heat and let the cherries soak in the syrup overnight at room temperature.

The day of serving, using an electric mixer, whip the cream while gradually adding the sugar until the cream forms medium peaks. Refrigerate.

Heat the crepe maker to 430°F (220°C) (or the skillet) and grease as directed. Pour and spread one-quarter (about $6\frac{1}{2}$ tbsp/100 mL) of the batter evenly. Cook, flipping, as directed. Brush the crepe with some of the melted butter. Use a spatula to fold the crepe into a fan shape, then place it folded side down on a plate.

Repeat the above steps for the other 3 crepes.

Spoon the cherry preserves on the crepe and add a quenelle of whipped cream in the middle.

Crepe with White Chocolate Sauce and Berries

MAKES 4 CREPES
PREPARATION: 10 MINUTES
COOKING TIME: 10 MINUTES

FOR THE WHITE CHOCOLATE SAUCE

- $3\frac{1}{2}$ oz (105 g) white chocolate
- $\frac{1}{4}$ cup (60 mL) heavy or whipping (35%) cream

FOR THE CREPES

- $1\frac{2}{3}$ cups (400 mL) crepe batter (see recipe on page 17)
- 3 tbsp (40 g) butter, melted
- 10 oz (300 g) berries (strawberries, raspberries, blackcurrants, redcurrants)

TIP

TO RETAIN THE TEXTURE OF WHITE CHOCOLATE, THE TEMPERATURE OF THE CHOCOLATE SHOULD NEVER EXCEED 122°F (50°C).

HOW TO FOLD

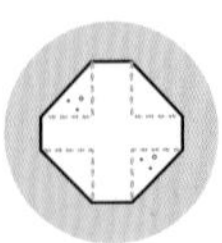

Make the sauce: Break the chocolate into pieces and melt it in the top of a double boiler set over simmering water. In a saucepan, heat the cream on low. Pour the warm cream over the melted chocolate and stir well until smooth. Set aside.

Heat the crepe maker to 430°F (220°C) (or the skillet) and grease as directed. Pour and spread one-quarter (about $6\frac{1}{2}$ tbsp/100 mL) of the batter evenly. Cook, flipping, as directed. Brush the crepe with some of the melted butter. Use a spatula to fold the crepe into an octagon, then place it folded side down on a plate.

Repeat the above steps for the other 3 crepes.

Brush each crepe with melted butter, drizzle with one-quarter of the white chocolate sauce, then gently place one-quarter of the berries on top.

MAKES 4 CREPES
PREPARATION: 20 MINUTES
COOKING TIME: 20 MINUTES

FOR THE PISTACHIO CREAM

- 6 tbsp (50 g) whole pistachios
- $\frac{3}{4}$ cup (175 mL) milk
- 1 egg
- $\frac{1}{4}$ cup (50 g) granulated sugar
- 2 tbsp (15 g) all-purpose flour

FOR THE CREPES

- $1\frac{2}{3}$ cups (400 mL) crepe batter (see recipe on page 17)
- 2 tbsp + 2 tsp (40 g) butter, melted
- 28 fresh raspberries

TIP

IF YOU MAKE THE PISTACHIO CREAM AHEAD OF TIME, PLACE THE PLASTIC WRAP DIRECTLY ON THE SURFACE OF THE CREAM SO IT DOESN'T DRY OUT.

HOW TO FOLD

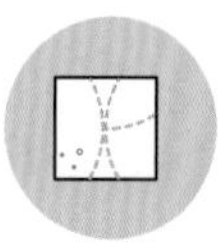

Pistachio Cream Crepe with Fresh Raspberries

Make the pistachio cream: In a blender, purée the pistachios and milk and pour it into a saucepan. Heat on low. In a large bowl, whisk together the egg and sugar until the mixture lightens in color. Whisk in the flour. Gradually add the warm milk mixture to the egg mixture while stirring. Return the mixture to the saucepan and cook on low, stirring with a wooden spoon, until thickened. Set aside.

Heat the crepe maker to 430°F (220°C) (or the skillet) and grease as directed. Pour and spread 6 tbsp (90 mL) of the batter evenly. Cook, flipping, as directed. Brush the crepe with some of the melted butter. Use the spatula to fold the crepe in a closed square, then place it folded side down on a plate.

Repeat the above steps for the other 3 crepes.

Brush each crepe with melted butter. Spoon one-quarter of the pistachio cream in the center of each crepe. Garnish with 7 raspberries.

Breizh Café farm is located in Saint-Coulomb, between Cancale and Saint-Malo, overlooking Duguesclin Bay.

This farm allows Atelier de la Crêpe interns to learn about agroforestry, respect for seasonal availability, sustainable agriculture and an ecological approach that respects local food networks.

Port of Saint-Malo (left) and Terre Nueve quay (right)

SUMMER RECIPES

MAKES 4 GALETTES
PREPARATION: 20 MINUTES
COOKING TIME: 10 MINUTES
RESTING TIME: 1 NIGHT IN THE FRIDGE

FOR THE SARDINE RILLETTES

- $^{1}/_{2}$ cup (120 g) butter
- $^{3}/_{4}$ cup (100 g) chopped shallots
- 1 cup + 6 tbsp (340 mL) heavy or whipping (35%) cream
- 8 oz (250 g) canned sardines
- 8 tsp (8 g) fresh chives

FOR THE GALETTES

- 2 cups (500 mL) galette batter (see recipe on page 15)
- 3 tbsp (40 g) butter, melted

TIPS

YOU CAN SERVE THIS GALETTE WITH A TOSSED SALAD (SEE RECIPE ON PAGE 26).

IF YOU PREFER A CRISPIER GALETTE, FLIP IT ON THE CREPE MAKER (OR SKILLET) TO COOK THE SECOND SIDE BEFORE ADDING THE FILLING.

HOW TO FOLD

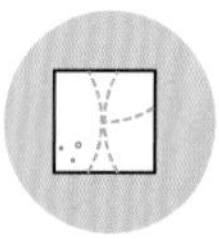

Galette with Sardine Rillettes

The day before, prepare the sardine rillettes: In a saucepan, melt the butter over medium heat. Add the shallots and sauté. Add the cream, reduce the heat to low and simmer until reduced by half. Place the drained sardines in a bowl and crush with a fork. Add the chives and mix well. Pour the creamed shallots over the sardines and stir. Let cool, cover, and refrigerate overnight.

The day of serving: Heat the crepe maker to 480°F (250°C) (or the skillet) and grease as directed. Pour and spread $^{1}/_{2}$ cup (125 mL) of the batter evenly. Brush the surface of the galette with some of the melted butter. Add one-quarter of the sardine rillettes and cook. When the edges start to lift, use the spatula to fold the galette into a closed square and turn it over. Brush the galette with melted butter.

Remove the galette from the crepe maker (or skillet) and serve it folded side down on a plate.

Repeat the above steps for the other 3 galettes.

MAKES 4 GALETTES
PREPARATION: 30 MINUTES
COOKING TIME: 20 MINUTES

FOR THE SUN-DRIED TOMATO COULIS

- 3 tbsp (50 g) drained oil-packed sun-dried tomatoes
- 5 tsp (25 mL) olive oil
- 1/4 cup (60 mL) water

FOR THE ROASTED PEPPERS

- 1 large (8 oz/250 g) green bell pepper
- 1 large (8 oz/250 g) yellow bell pepper
- 1 large (8 oz/250 g) red bell pepper

FOR THE GALETTES

- 2 cups (500 mL) galette batter (see recipe on page 15)
- 2 tbsp + 2 tsp (40 g) butter, melted
- 1 cup (120 g) grated Emmental cheese
- 4 oz (125 g) cured chorizo sausage, cut in rounds

TIP

COVERING THE PEPPERS TIGHTLY WITH FOIL MAKES THEM EASIER TO PEEL.

HOW TO FOLD

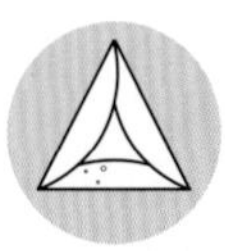

Chorizo, Emmental and Roasted Pepper Galette

with Sun-Dried Tomato Coulis

Make the sun-dried tomato coulis: In a blender, combine the sun-dried tomatoes, oil and water. Purée until just slightly chunky but not smooth. Transfer to a bowl, cover and chill until ready to use.

Prepare the roasted peppers: Preheat the oven to 350°F (180°C). Cut the peppers in half and remove the seeds. Place the peppers on a baking sheet and roast for 10 minutes, until browned. Remove from the oven, cover with foil and let cool. Peel the peppers and cut them into strips.

Heat the crepe maker to 480°F (250°C) (or the skillet) and grease as directed. Pour and spread 1/2 cup (125 mL) of the batter evenly. Brush the galette with some of the melted butter. Sprinkle one-quarter of the Emmental in the center. Add one-quarter of each of the peppers and the chorizo and cook. When the edges start to lift, use the spatula to fold the galette into an open triangle. Brush the folds of the galette with melted butter.

Remove the galette from the crepe maker (or skillet) and serve it on a plate.

Repeat the above steps for the other 3 galettes.

Drizzle each galette with one-quarter of the sun-dried tomato coulis.

MAKES 4 GALETTES

PREPARATION: 30 MINUTES

COOKING TIME: 20 MINUTES

RESTING TIME: 15 MINUTES IN THE FRIDGE

Galette with Seasonal Vegetables, Capicola and Basil Sauce

FOR THE BASIL SAUCE

- 2 cups (100 g) fresh basil leaves
- 1 garlic clove
- $1\frac{2}{3}$ cups (400 mL) oil
- 1 pinch of salt

FOR THE VEGETABLES

- 1 small eggplant
- 1 small zucchini
- Olive oil
- Salt and pepper
- 1 tomato

FOR THE GALETTES

- 2 cups (500 mL) galette batter (see recipe on page 15)
- 3 tbsp (40 g) butter, melted
- 1 cup (120 g) grated Emmental cheese
- 4 oz (125 g) sliced capicola

Make the basil sauce: In a blender or food processor, combine the basil leaves, garlic, oil and salt. Purée until smooth. Refrigerate for 15 minutes.

Prepare the vegetables: Cut the eggplant and zucchini into $\frac{1}{4}$-inch (5 mm) slices. (Cook the eggplant as soon as you cut it into disks so it doesn't turn brown.) Sauté each vegetable separately in olive oil. Season with salt and pepper. Remove from the heat. Cut the tomato into $\frac{1}{4}$-inch (5 mm) slices and add to the skillet (do not cook). Season with salt and pepper.

Heat the crepe maker to 480°F (250°C) (or the skillet). Pour and spread $\frac{1}{2}$ cup (125 mL) of the batter evenly. Brush the galette with some of the melted butter. Sprinkle one-quarter of the grated Emmental, then add one-quarter of the eggplant, zucchini and tomato and cook. When the edges start to lift, use the spatula to fold the galette into an open square (full fold). Brush the folded edges of the galette with melted butter.

Remove the galette from the crepe maker (or skillet) and serve it on a plate.

Repeat the above steps for the other 3 galettes.

Garnish each galette with 2 tbsp (30 mL) basil sauce and top with capicola.

TIP

ANY EXTRA EGGPLANT AND ZUCCHINI CAN BE SERVED ON A SIDE SALAD OR RESERVED FOR ANOTHER USE.

EXTRA BASIL SAUCE CAN BE STORED IN THE FRIDGE UP TO 2 DAYS OR FROZEN FOR 3 MONTHS.

HOW TO FOLD

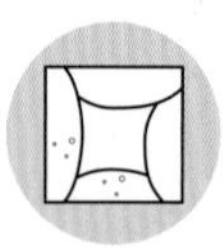

MAKES 4 GALETTES
PREPARATION: 15 MINUTES
COOKING TIME: 50 MINUTES

FOR THE RATATOUILLE

- 6 tbsp + 2 tsp (100 mL) olive oil, divided, plus more as needed
- 1 cup (130 g) chopped onion
- $2\frac{3}{4}$ cups (500 g) diced tomatoes
- $\frac{3}{4}$ cup (130 g) chopped mixed yellow, red and green bell peppers
- 1 garlic clove, chopped
- Salt
- Pepper
- $1\frac{1}{2}$ cups (125 g) cubed ($\frac{1}{2}$-inch/1 cm) eggplant
- 1 cup (125 g) cubed ($\frac{1}{2}$-inch/1 cm) zucchini

FOR THE GALETTES

- 2 cups (500 mL) galette batter (see recipe on page 15)
- $\frac{1}{3}$ cup (80 g) butter, melted
- 4 oz (125 g) soft goat cheese
- 4 oz (125 g) thinly sliced prosciutto

HOW TO FOLD

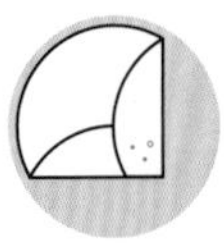

RATATOUILLE, GOAT CHEESE AND HAM GALETTE

Make the ratatouille: In a saucepan, heat 2 tsp (10 mL) of olive oil over high heat and sauté the onions. Add the tomatoes. Cover and simmer over low heat. In a skillet, heat the remaining olive oil over high heat and sauté the bell peppers with the garlic. Season with salt and pepper. Do the same with the eggplant and zucchini, separately. Combine all the vegetables in the saucepan with the tomatoes. Stir and simmer for around 20 minutes, until slightly thickened.

Heat the crepe maker to 480°F (250°C) (or the skillet) and grease as directed. Pour and spread $\frac{1}{2}$ cup (125 mL) of the batter evenly. Brush the galette with some of the melted butter. Spoon one-quarter of the ratatouille and one-quarter of the goat cheese into the center and cook. When the edges start to lift, use the spatula to fold the galette into a fan shape. Brush the folded edges of the galette with melted butter.

Remove the galette from the crepe maker (or skillet) and serve it on a plate. Place one-quarter of the prosciutto on the galette.

Repeat the above steps for the other 3 galettes.

MAKES 1 GALETTE ROLL

PREPARATION: 15 MINUTES
COOKING TIME: 2 MINUTES
RESTING TIME: 30 MINUTES IN THE FRIDGE

- $^{1}/_{2}$ cup (125 mL) galette batter (see recipe on page 15)
- 2 tsp (10 g) butter, melted
- $1^{3}/_{4}$ oz (50 g) soft goat cheese
- 2 tbsp (30 g) finely chopped oil-packed sun-dried tomatoes

TIP

COOK THE SECOND SIDE OF THE GALETTE FOR LESS TIME THAN THE FIRST SIDE.

HOW TO FOLD

Galette Roll

with Goat Cheese and Sun-Dried Tomatoes

Heat the crepe maker to 480°F (250°C) (or the skillet) and grease as directed. Pour and spread the batter evenly. Brush the galette with melted butter. Cook for a few seconds, until the edges lift, then flip over the galette to cook the second side, just until dry. Use a spatula to remove the galette from the crepe maker and let cool on a rack.

With a teaspoon, make small scoops of the goat cheese and place them in a line down the center of the galette. Place the sun-dried tomatoes on the goat cheese.

Roll up the galette tightly and wrap it in plastic wrap. Refrigerate for 30 minutes.

Unwrap and cut the roll into bite-size pieces and arrange them on a plate.

MAKES 4 CREPES

PREPARATION: 20 MINUTES

COOKING TIME: 20 MINUTES

RESTING TIME: 30 MINUTES IN THE FRIDGE

FOR THE COCONUT CREAM

- 3 tbsp + 1 tsp (50 g) butter, melted
- $\frac{1}{4}$ cup (50 g) granulated sugar
- 1 pasteurized egg
- $\frac{1}{2}$ cup (50 g) shredded sweetened coconut

FOR THE CHOCOLATE SAUCE

- $1\frac{3}{4}$ oz (50 g) dark chocolate
- $\frac{1}{3}$ cup (75 mL) heavy or whipping (35%) cream

FOR THE CREPES

- $1\frac{2}{3}$ cups (400 mL) crepe batter (see recipe on page 17)
- 3 tbsp (40 g) butter, melted
- Shredded sweetened coconut

TIP

THIS RECIPE CONTAINS RAW EGGS. IF YOU ARE CONCERNED ABOUT THE FOOD SAFETY OF A RAW EGG, SUBSTITUTE PASTEURIZED EGGS IN THE SHELL OR $\frac{1}{4}$ CUP (60 ML) PASTEURIZED LIQUID WHOLE EGGS.

HOW TO FOLD

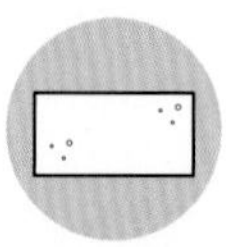

Coconut Cream Crepe

with Chocolate Sauce and Grated Coconut

Make the coconut cream: Mix the melted butter with the sugar using a flexible spatula (don't use a whisk, as it will add air to the mixture). Incorporate the egg. Add the shredded coconut and mix well. Cover and refrigerate for 30 minutes.

Make the chocolate sauce: Break the chocolate into a heatproof bowl and set over a saucepan of hot water to melt. In another saucepan, heat the cream gently. When it is warm, pour it into the chocolate and stir until smooth. Set aside.

Heat the crepe maker to 430°F (220°C) (or the skillet) and grease as directed. Pour and spread one-quarter (about $6\frac{1}{2}$ tbsp/100 mL) of the batter evenly. Cook, flipping the crepe, as directed. Brush the crepe with some of the melted butter. Add one-quarter of the coconut cream in the center. Use the spatula to fold the crepe into a rectangle, then serve it gently on a plate.

Repeat the above steps for the other 3 crepes.

Brush each crepe with melted butter, decorate with one-quarter of the chocolate sauce in a lattice design, and sprinkle with one-quarter of the shredded coconut.

Rhubarb Compote Crepe

with Strawberry Coulis

MAKES 4 CREPES

PREPARATION: 20 MINUTES

COOKING TIME: 20 MINUTES

RESTING TIME: 1 NIGHT IN THE FRIDGE

FOR THE RHUBARB COMPOTE

- 1 lb (500 g) rhubarb
- $\frac{1}{2}$ cup (100 g) superfine granulated sugar

FOR THE STRAWBERRY COULIS

- $\frac{2}{3}$ cup (100 g) strawberries
- $2\frac{1}{2}$ tbsp (30 g) superfine granulated sugar
- $\frac{3}{4}$ tsp (3 mL) lemon juice

FOR THE CREPES

- 8 strawberries
- $1\frac{2}{3}$ cups (400 mL) crepe batter (see recipe on page 17)
- 4 tsp (20 g) butter, melted

TIP

THE MORE ACIDIC THE RHUBARB IS, THE MORE SUGAR YOU NEED TO ADD. ADD MORE, IF NECESSARY, AFTER COOKING THE COMPOTE.

HOW TO FOLD

The day before, make the rhubarb compote: Peel the rhubarb and cut it into $\frac{3}{4}$-inch (2 cm) cubes. Combine the rhubarb and sugar in a container and chill overnight in the fridge.

The day of serving, strain the rhubarb juice into a saucepan, reserving the rhubarb. Simmer the juice over low heat until reduced and syrupy. Then add the rhubarb and simmer until softened. Set aside.

Make the strawberry coulis: Hull the strawberries. In a blender, purée the strawberries with the sugar and lemon juice. Strain the mixture through a fine fine-mesh sieve. Set aside.

Cut the 8 strawberries into small cubes.

Heat the crepe maker to 430°F (220°C) (or the skillet) and grease as directed. Pour and spread one-quarter (about $6\frac{1}{2}$ tbsp/100 mL) of the batter evenly. Cook, flipping the crepe, as directed. Brush the crepe with some of the melted butter. Place the crepe on a plate.

Repeat the above steps for the other 3 crepes, stacking the crepes on the plate.

Add one-quarter of the rhubarb compote to center of a crepe. Fold the crepe into a beggar's purse shape, then place it gently on another plate. Pour one-quarter of the coulis around it and add one-quarter of the cubed strawberries. Repeat with the other 3 crepes.

ATELIER
DE LA
CRÊPE

Nectarine Compote Crepe

with Raspberry Coulis

MAKES 4 CREPES
Preparation: 20 minutes
Cooking time: 30 minutes

FOR THE NECTARINE COMPOTE

- 2 lbs (1 kg) nectarines
- 4 tsp (20 mL) water

FOR THE RASPBERRY COULIS

- 3 tbsp (40 g) superfine granulated sugar
- 2 tbsp + 2 tsp (40 mL) water
- $\frac{3}{4}$ cup (100 g) raspberries

FOR THE CREPES

- $1\frac{2}{3}$ cups (400 mL) crepe batter (see recipe on page 17)
- 3 tbsp (40 g) butter, melted
- 1 nectarine, thinly sliced

TIP

TO PEEL NECTARINES EASILY, PLUNGE THEM INTO BOILING WATER FOR 30 SECONDS, THEN PUT THEM IN ICE WATER FOR 30 SECONDS.

HOW TO FOLD

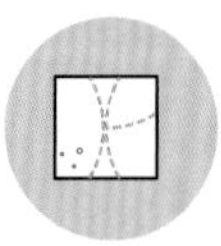

Make the nectarine compote: Peel the nectarines and remove the pits, then cut each in quarters. Place them in a saucepan with water and simmer over low heat until the nectarines are tender, adding a small amount of water if the mixture is too dry while cooking. Set aside.

Make the raspberry coulis: Heat the sugar and water in a saucepan to dissolve the sugar. Add the raspberries and stir. Purée in a blender until smooth. Set aside.

Heat the crepe maker to 430°F (220°C) (or the skillet) and grease as directed. Pour and spread one-quarter (about $6\frac{1}{2}$ tbsp/100 mL) of the batter evenly. Cook, flipping the crepe, as directed. Brush the crepe with some of the melted butter. Place one-quarter of the nectarine compote on the galette. Use the spatula to fold the crepe into a closed square, then serve it folded side down on a plate.

Repeat the above steps for the other 3 crepes.

Drizzle each crepe with raspberry coulis and garnish with thin slices of nectarine.

MAKES 4 CREPES

PREPARATION: 20 MINUTES

COOKING TIME: 20 MINUTES

FOR THE RUM CARAMELIZED PINEAPPLE

- 1 small pineapple
- 7 tbsp (100 g) butter
- 1 cup (200 g) granulated sugar
- $\frac{1}{3}$ cup (75 mL) heavy or whipping (35%) cream
- 4 tsp (20 mL) rum

FOR THE CREPES

- $1\frac{2}{3}$ cups (400 mL) crepe batter (see recipe on page 17)
- 3 tbsp (40 g) butter, melted
- Shredded sweetened coconut

TIPS

IF YOU PREFER AN ALCOHOL-FREE CREPE, REPLACE THE RUM WITH PINEAPPLE JUICE.

STORE EXTRA CARAMELIZED PINEAPPLE IN THE REFRIGERATOR FOR UP TO 5 DAYS. REHEAT TO SERVE MORE CREPES OR SERVE ON ICE CREAM.

HOW TO FOLD

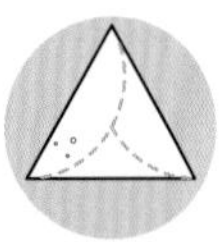

Caramelized Pineapple Crepe

with Rum and Shredded Coconut

Prepare the pineapple: Peel and cut into quarters. Remove the core and cut the flesh into $\frac{3}{4}$-inch (2 cm) chunks.

In a skillet, melt the butter over high heat. Add the sugar and pineapple chunks. Cook until the fruit is caramelized on both sides. Pour in the cream and the rum to stop the caramelization. Set aside.

Heat the crepe maker to 430°F (220°C) (or the skillet) and grease as directed. Pour and spread one-quarter (about $6\frac{1}{2}$ tbsp/100 mL) of the batter evenly. Cook, flipping the crepe, as directed. Brush the crepe with some of the melted butter. Use the spatula to fold the crepe into a triangle, then serve it folded side down on a plate.

Repeat the above steps for the other 3 crepes.

Reheat the caramelized pineapple for a few seconds, place 3 pieces on each crepe and drizzle with caramelized juice. Sprinkle with shredded coconut and serve more pineapple on the side as desired.

Grapefruit and Ginger-Salted Caramel Crepe

MAKES 4 CREPES
PREPARATION: 30 MINUTES
COOKING TIME: 55 MINUTES
RESTING TIME: 1 NIGHT IN THE FRIDGE

FOR THE GINGER SYRUP

- 2 tbsp (25 g) grated peeled ginger root (2- by 1-inch/ 5 by 2.5 cm piece)
- 2 tbsp (25 g) superfine granulated sugar
- 1 tsp (5 mL) lemon juice
- $\frac{1}{4}$ cup (60 mL) water

FOR THE CANDIED GINGER

- $3\frac{1}{2}$ oz (105 g) ginger root
- 1 cup (250 mL) water
- $\frac{1}{2}$ cup (100 g) granulated sugar
- 1 dash of lemon juice

FOR THE SALTED CARAMEL

- 3 tbsp + 1 tsp (50 g) salted butter
- $\frac{1}{3}$ cup (60 g) granulated sugar
- 4 tsp (20 mL) water
- $\frac{1}{4}$ cup (60 mL) heavy or whipping (35%) cream

FOR THE CREPES

- $1\frac{2}{3}$ cups (400 mL) crepe batter (see recipe on page 17)
- 3 tbsp (40 g) butter, melted
- 20 grapefruit segments

HOW TO FOLD

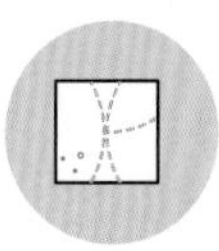

The day before, prepare the ginger for the syrup: In a bowl, stir the ginger and sugar, cover and let soak at room temperature overnight so the ginger releases its liquid.

The day before, prepare the candied ginger: Cut the ginger into long strips using a mandolin. Blanch for 2 minutes in boiling water, then drain. Make a syrup in a saucepan with the water, sugar and a dash of lemon juice. Add the ginger strips and cook for 10 minutes until softened. Let cool for a few minutes, cover and refrigerate overnight.

The day of serving, place the grated ginger mixture in a saucepan and add the lemon juice. Simmer for 20 minutes over low heat, until the ginger is transparent. Strain through a fine-mesh sieve and discard the solids.

Make the salted caramel: Melt the butter in a saucepan. Add the sugar and 4 tsp (20 mL) water. Stir and cook over high heat until a caramel forms. Remove from the heat. Heat the cream on low in a small saucepan, then pour it over the caramel.

Add the ginger syrup to the salted caramel and stir.

Heat the crepe maker to 430°F (220°C) (or the skillet) and grease as directed. Pour and spread one-quarter (about $6\frac{1}{2}$ tbsp/100 mL) of the batter evenly. Cook, flipping the crepe, as directed. Brush the crepe with some of the melted butter. Use the spatula to fold the crepe into a closed square, then serve it folded side down on a plate.

Repeat the above steps for the other 3 crepes.

Brush the crepes with melted butter. For each crepe, add 5 grapefruit segments in a star shape, then add one-quarter of the ginger caramel. Add a few slices of candied ginger in the middle.

Granite, untreated wood, slate: Breizh Café's decor sets the stage. One of the first Breizh Café crepe restaurants — it opened in Cancale in 2005 — is at 7 quai Administrateur Chef Thomas. Le Comptoir Breizh Café is at 6, rue de l'Orme in Saint-Malo.

In Breizh Café restaurants, you can try as many crepes and organic buckwheat galettes as you like, with a wide range of ciders. Breizh Café is an official partner of Atelier de la Crêpe.

BREIZH Café
CRÊPERIE

Sillon Beach in Saint-Malo

FALL RECIPES

MAKES 4 GALETTES
PREPARATION: 20 MINUTES
COOKING TIME: 30 MINUTES

FOR THE APPLESAUCE

- 2 lbs (1 kg) apples
- $^{3}/_{4}$ cup + 5 tsp (200 mL) water

FOR THE GALETTES

- 16 slices Andouille sausage
- 2 cups (500 mL) galette batter (see recipe on page 15)
- 3 tbsp (40 g) butter, melted

HOW TO FOLD

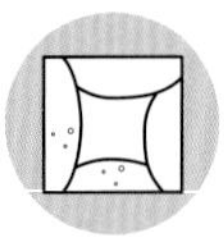

Applesauce and Grilled Andouille Galette

Make the applesauce: Peel the apples, cut in quarters and remove the cores. In a saucepan, combine the water and apples and simmer over low heat, stirring occasionally, until the apples fall apart (but do not purée them). Set aside.

Sear the andouille slices in a hot skillet or on a plancha. Set aside.

Heat the crepe maker to 480°F (250°C) (or the skillet) and grease as directed. Pour and spread $^{1}/_{2}$ cup (125 mL) of the batter evenly. Brush the galette with some of the melted butter. Place one-quarter of the applesauce in the center, add 4 slices of the grilled andouille and cook. When the edges start to lift, use the spatula to fold the galette into an open square (full fold). Brush the folded edges of the galette with melted butter.

Use the spatula to serve the galette on a plate.

Repeat the above steps for the other 3 galettes.

Bleu d'Auvergne Galette

with Fried Pears and Pine Nuts

MAKES 4 GALETTES
PREPARATION: 15 MINUTES
COOKING TIME: 15 MINUTES

FOR THE FRIED PEARS

- 1 lb (500 g) pears
- $2\frac{1}{2}$ tbsp (38 g) butter
- $1\frac{1}{2}$ tbsp (20 g) granulated sugar

FOR THE GALETTES

- 2 cups (500 mL) galette batter (see recipe on page 15)
- 3 tbsp (40 g) butter, melted
- 7 oz (210 g) Bleu d'Auvergne or other French blue cheese, crumbled
- $\frac{1}{3}$ cup (40 g) pine nuts

TIP

YOU CAN REPLACE THE PINE NUTS WITH THE NUTS OF YOUR CHOICE.

HOW TO FOLD

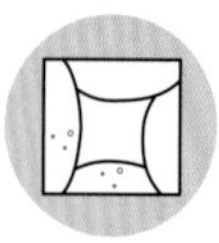

Prepare the fried pears: Peel the pears, remove the cores, then cut them into slices. Brown them in a skillet in the butter, then add the sugar and cook until caramelized.

Heat the crepe maker to 480°F (250°C) (or the skillet) and grease as directed. Pour and spread $\frac{1}{2}$ cup (125 mL) of the batter evenly. Brush the galette with some of the melted butter. Place one-quarter of the crumbled blue cheese in the center. Add one-quarter of the fried pears and cook. When the edges start to lift, use the spatula to fold the galette into an open square (full fold). Brush the folded edges of the galette with melted butter. Cook until the cheese is completely melted.

Use the spatula to serve the galette on a plate. Sprinkle with one-quarter of the pine nuts.

Repeat the above steps for the other 3 galettes.

MAKES 4 GALETTES

PREPARATION: 30 MINUTES

COOKING TIME: 25 MINUTES

RESTING TIME: 1 NIGHT IN THE FRIDGE

FOR THE GRAPE JAM

- 1 cup (160 g) grapes
- 1 dash of lemon juice
- $1\frac{1}{2}$ tbsp (30 g) honey
- $2\frac{1}{2}$ tbsp (30 g) granulated sugar

FOR THE GALETTES

- 2 cups (500 mL) galette batter (see recipe on page 15)
- 3 tbsp (40 g) butter, melted
- 7 oz (210 g) soft goat cheese
- $\frac{1}{3}$ cup (40 g) nuts, chopped

TIP

IT'S IMPORTANT TO LET THE GRAPES STAND LONG ENOUGH TO RELEASE ALL THEIR JUICE WHICH IS WHY IT'S BEST TO START THE DAY BEFORE MAKING THE JAM.

HOW TO FOLD

Goat Cheese Galette

with Grape Jam

The day before serving, make the grape jam: Cut the grapes in half and remove the seeds. Put the grapes in a large bowl, then stir in the lemon juice, honey and sugar. Cover and refrigerate overnight to let the grapes release their juice.

The day of serving, place the grapes and their juice in a saucepan and cook for about 20 minutes. Strain the mixture through a fine-mesh sieve to remove any remaining seeds and then purée slightly in a blender or mini food processor.

Heat the crepe maker to 480°F (250°C) (or the skillet) and grease as directed. Pour and spread $\frac{1}{2}$ cup (125 mL) of the batter evenly. Brush the galette with some of the melted butter. Place one-quarter of the goat cheese in the center and cook. When the edges start to lift, use the spatula to fold the galette into an open triangle. Brush the folded edges of the galette with melted butter. Use the spatula to serve the galette on a plate.

Repeat the above steps for the other 3 galettes.

For each galette, pour one-quarter of the grape jam in a circle and sprinkle with one-quarter of the chopped nuts.

MAKES 4 GALETTES

PREPARATION: 20 MINUTES

COOKING TIME: 15 MINUTES

RESTING TIME: 6 HOURS IN THE FRIDGE

FOR THE CIDER JELLY

- $\frac{1}{4}$ tsp (1.5 g) agar-agar
- $6\frac{1}{2}$ tbsp (100 mL) apple juice, divided
- $6\frac{1}{2}$ tbsp (100 mL) dry cider
- $\frac{1}{4}$ cup (50 g) granulated sugar

FOR THE GALETTES

- 2 cups (500 mL) galette batter (see recipe on page 15)
- 3 tbsp (40 g) butter, melted
- 7 oz (210 g) Camembert cheese, thinly sliced

FOR THE SALAD

- $4\frac{1}{2}$ cups (160 g) salad greens
- Cider vinaigrette (see recipe on page 26)
- 5 oz (150 g) thinly sliced prosciutto

TIPS

IF YOU MAKE THE JELLY WITH SWEET CIDER, OMIT THE SUGAR FROM THE RECIPE.

STORE ANY EXTRA CIDER JELLY IN A JAR IN THE REFRIGERATOR FOR UP TO 1 MONTH.

HOW TO FOLD

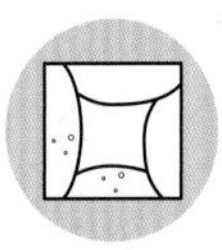

CAMEMBERT GALETTE

WITH CIDER JELLY, CURED HAM AND SALAD GREENS

Make the cider jelly: In a bowl, mix the agar-agar with 1 tbsp (15 mL) apple juice. Heat the cider, the remaining apple juice and sugar in a saucepan over high heat. When the mixture comes to a boil, reduce the heat to low and add the diluted agar-agar. Whisk. Pour the mixture into a glass jar and let cool. Cover and refrigerate for about 6 hours, until set.

Heat the crepe maker to 480°F (250°C) (or the skillet) and grease as directed. Pour and spread $\frac{1}{2}$ cup (125 mL) of the batter evenly. Brush the galette with some of the melted butter. Place one-quarter of the thinly sliced Camembert in the center. Add 2 tbsp (40 g) cider jelly and cook. When the edges start to lift, use the spatula to fold the galette into an open square (full fold). Brush the folded edges of the galette with melted butter. Cook until the cheese is melted. Use the spatula to serve the galette on a plate.

Repeat the above steps for the other 3 galettes.

Dress the salad with the cider vinaigrette. Place one-quarter of the salad on each of the galettes. Arrange one-quarter of the prosciutto on the top of each galette.

MAKES 4 GALETTES
PREPARATION: 20 MINUTES
COOKING TIME: 40 MINUTES

FOR THE APPLESAUCE

- 1 lb 7 oz (710 g) apples
- 3/4 cup + 5 tsp (200 mL) water

FOR THE FRIED APPLES

- 3 apples
- 2 tbsp + 1 tsp (35 g) butter

FOR THE GALETTES

- 14 oz (435 g) black pudding
- 2 cups (500 mL) galette batter (see recipe on page 15)
- 3 tbsp (40 g) butter, melted

HOW TO FOLD

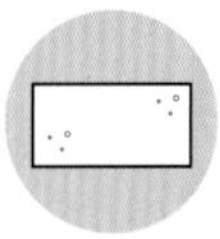

Black Pudding Galette

with Applesauce and Fried Apples

Make the applesauce: Peel and core the apples, then cut them into quarters. In a saucepan, combine the water and quartered apples and simmer over low heat, stirring occasionally, until the apples fall apart (but do not purée). Set aside.

Make the fried apples: Peel and core the apples, then cut them into quarters. Sauté the apples in butter in a skillet until they are browned but the centers are still firm. Set them aside on a plate.

Using two large spoons, form 8 quenelles of black pudding, then cook them gently in the skillet. Set aside.

Heat the crepe maker to 480°F (250°C) (or the skillet) and grease as directed. Pour and spread 1/2 cup (125 mL) of the batter evenly. Brush the galette with some of the melted butter. Add one-quarter of the applesauce and cook. When the edges start to lift, use the spatula to fold the galette into a closed rectangle. Brush the galette with melted butter. Flip the galette and cook. Use the spatula to serve the galette with the folded side down on a plate.

Repeat the above steps for the other 3 galettes.

Top each galette with 2 quenelles of black pudding and 3 fried apple quarters.

MAKES 4 GALETTES
PREPARATION: 20 MINUTES
COOKING TIME: 15 MINUTES

FOR THE FRIED APPLES

- 1 lb (500 g) apples
- 2 tbsp (30 g) butter

FOR THE GALETTES

- 2 cups (500 mL) galette batter (see recipe on page 15)
- 3 tbsp (40 g) butter, melted
- 8 oz (250 g) Curé Nantais cheese or other soft, washed-rind cheese

FOR THE SALAD

- $4\frac{1}{2}$ cups (160 g) salad greens
- Cider vinaigrette (see recipe on page 26)

HOW TO FOLD

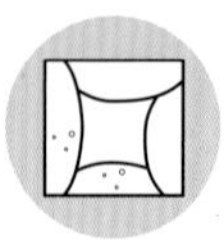

CURÉ NANTAIS GALETTE

WITH FRIED APPLES AND SALAD

Prepare the fried apples: Peel and core the apples, then dice. Sauté them in butter in a skillet. The insides should be firm and the outsides should be browned.

Heat the crepe maker to 480°F (250°C) (or the skillet) and grease as directed. Pour and spread $\frac{1}{2}$ cup (125 mL) of the batter evenly. Brush the surface of the galette with some of the melted butter. Place one-quarter of the cheese in the center. Add one-quarter of the fried apples and cook. When the edges start to lift, use the spatula to fold the galette into an open square (full fold). Brush the folded edges of the galette with melted butter. Cook until the cheese is melted. Use the spatula to gently place the galette on a serving plate.

Repeat the above steps for the other 3 galettes.

Dress the salad greens with the cider vinaigrette. Arrange one-quarter of the salad in a circle on top of each galette.

MAKES 1 GALETTE ROLL

PREPARATION: 10 MINUTES
COOKING TIME: 2 MINUTES
RESTING TIME: 30 MINUTES IN THE FRIDGE

FOR THE MUSTARD BUTTER

- 2 tbsp (30 g) butter (at room temperature)
- 1 tbsp (15 g) whole-grain mustard

FOR THE GALETTES

- ½ cup (125 mL) galette batter (see recipe on page 15)
- 1½ oz (45 g) deli smoked ham, sliced

TIP

SERVE THE ROLL 1 TO 2 HOURS AFTER PREPARING IT FOR THE SMOOTHEST TEXTURE.

HOW TO FOLD

GALETTE ROLL

WITH HAM AND MUSTARD BUTTER

Make the mustard butter: Combine the soft butter and mustard.

Heat the crepe maker to 480°F (250°C) (or the skillet) and grease as directed. Pour and spread the batter evenly. Cook, flipping the galette, as directed. When the edges start to lift, use a spatula to place the galette on a cutting board.

Spread the mustard butter over the entire surface of the galette. Place the ham in the center, then roll up the galette tightly.

Wrap the roll in plastic wrap and refrigerate for 30 minutes, until the mustard butter hardens.

Unwrap, cut the roll in bite-size pieces and serve on a plate.

MAKES 4 CREPES

PREPARATION: 20 MINUTES

COOKING TIME: 20 MINUTES

RESTING TIME: 1 NIGHT IN THE FRIDGE

FOR THE CALVADOS RAISINS

- $^{2}/_{3}$ cup (100 g) raisins
- $^{3}/_{4}$ cup + 5 tsp (200 mL) Calvados

FOR THE APPLESAUCE

- 1 lb 7 oz (710 g) apples
- $^{3}/_{4}$ cup + 5 tsp (200 mL) water

FOR THE CREPES

- 1$^{2}/_{3}$ cups (400 mL) crepe batter (see recipe on page 17)
- 3 tbsp (40 g) butter, melted
- 4 scoops vanilla ice cream

TIP

IF THERE ISN'T ENOUGH CALVADOS IN THE RAISINS AFTER SOAKING, ADD MORE BOILED CALVADOS TO MAKE A SAUCE.

HOW TO FOLD

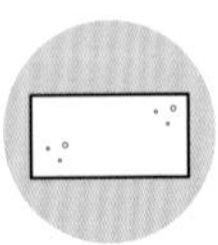

Applesauce and Calvados Raisin Crepe

The day before, prepare the raisins: Place the raisins in a saucepan, add the Calvados and bring to a boil. When the Calvados starts to boil, remove the pan from the heat and let cool. Cover and refrigerate overnight so the raisins can soak up the Calvados.

The day of serving, make the applesauce: Peel and core the apples, then cut them into quarters. Place the water and quartered apples in a saucepan and simmer over low heat, stirring occasionally, until the apples fall apart (but do not purée).

Heat the crepe maker to 430°F (220°C) (or the skillet) and grease as directed. Pour and spread one-quarter (about 6$^{1}/_{2}$ tbsp/100 mL) of the batter evenly. Cook, flipping the crepe, as directed. Brush the crepe with some of the melted butter. Place one-quarter of the applesauce in the middle. Use the spatula to fold the crepe into a rectangle, flip it over and serve it on a plate.

Repeat the above steps for the other 3 crepes.

Brush the crepes with melted butter and top each one with one-quarter of the Calvados raisins. Add a scoop of ice cream on top.

Mashed Banana Crepe

with Ginger-Chocolate Sauce

MAKES 4 CREPES
PREPARATION: 30 MINUTES
COOKING TIME: 30 MINUTES
RESTING TIME: 1 NIGHT

FOR THE GINGER SYRUP

- 2 tbsp (25 g) grated peeled ginger root (2- by 1-inch/5 by 2.5 cm piece)
- 2 tbsp (25 g) superfine granulated sugar
- 1 tsp (5 mL) lemon juice
- $\frac{1}{4}$ cup (60 mL) water

FOR THE CHOCOLATE SAUCE

- $1\frac{3}{4}$ oz (50 g) dark chocolate
- $\frac{1}{4}$ cup (60 mL) heavy or whipping (35%) cream
- 4 tsp (20 mL) water (optional)

FOR THE CREPES

- $1\frac{2}{3}$ cups (400 mL) crepe batter (see recipe on page 17)
- 4 ripe bananas
- 3 tbsp (40 g) butter, melted
- Banana slices

TIP

USE VERY RIPE BANANAS FOR THIS RECIPE. IF THE BANANAS ARE NOT RIPE ENOUGH, FRY THEM IN BUTTER INSTEAD OF MASHING THEM.

HOW TO FOLD

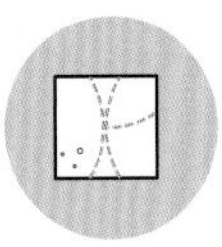

The night before, make the syrup: In a bowl, stir the ginger and sugar and let it sit overnight at room temperature so the ginger releases its liquid.

The day of serving, place the ginger mixture in a saucepan and add the lemon juice and water. Simmer for 20 minutes over low heat, until the ginger is transparent.

Make the chocolate sauce: Break the chocolate into pieces, place them in a heatproof bowl and set over a saucepan of hot water to melt. In a small saucepan, heat the cream on low. Pour the warm cream into the melted chocolate and stir well until smooth. Add the ginger syrup. Add a little water if the sauce is too thick. Set aside.

Peel and mash each of the 4 ripe bananas separately.

Heat the crepe maker to 430°F (220°C) (or the skillet) and grease as directed. Pour and spread one-quarter (about $6\frac{1}{2}$ tbsp/100 mL) of the batter evenly. Cook, flipping the crepe, as directed. Brush the crepe with some of the melted butter. Place 1 mashed banana in the center, then use the spatula to fold the crepe into a closed square. Place it folded side down on a plate.

Repeat the above steps for the other 3 crepes.

Brush the crepes with melted butter, garnish with banana slices and top with chocolate-ginger sauce.

ATELIER
DE LA CRÊPE
SAINT-MALO

MAKES 4 CREPES

PREPARATION: 15 MINUTES

COOKING TIME: 25 MINUTES

RESTING TIME: 1 NIGHT IN THE FRIDGE

FOR THE POACHED PEARS

- 2 pears
- 1 cup (250 mL) water
- 2 tsp (10 mL) lemon juice
- 10 tbsp (120 g) granulated sugar

FOR THE CHOCOLATE SAUCE

- $1\frac{3}{4}$ oz (50 g) dark chocolate
- $\frac{1}{3}$ cup (75 mL) heavy or whipping (35%) cream

FOR THE CREPES

- $1\frac{2}{3}$ cups (400 mL) crepe batter (see recipe on page 17)
- 3 tbsp (40 g) butter, melted

TIP

YOU CAN GARNISH THE POACHED PEARS WITH PLAIN, SPICED OR GINGER SALTED CARAMEL.

HOW TO FOLD

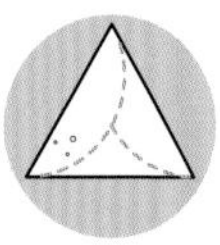

POACHED PEAR CREPE

WITH CHOCOLATE SAUCE

The day before, prepare the poached pears: Peel and core the pears, then cut them in half lengthwise. In a saucepan, combine the water, lemon juice and sugar and bring to a boil. Add the pear halves and cook for 10 minutes, just until tender (adjust the timing based on how ripe the fruit is). Remove the pan from the heat and let cool. Cover and refrigerate overnight. Let warm to room temperature before serving.

The day of serving, make the chocolate sauce: Break the chocolate into pieces, place them in a heatproof bowl and set it over a saucepan of hot water to melt. In a saucepan, warm the cream. Pour it over the melted chocolate and stir until smooth. Set aside.

Heat the crepe maker to 430°F (220°C) (or the skillet) and grease as directed. Pour and spread one-quarter (about $6\frac{1}{2}$ tbsp/100 mL) of the batter evenly. Cook, flipping the crepe, as directed. Brush the crepe with some of the melted butter. Use the spatula to fold the crepe into a triangle then serve it folded side down on a plate.

Repeat the above steps for the other 3 crepes.

Remove the pears from the liquid. Cut the pear halves into thin slices and arrange one-quarter of the slices in a circle in the middle of each crepe. Drizzle one-quarter of the chocolate sauce in circles around the pears.

MAKES 4 CREPES

PREPARATION: 15 MINUTES

COOKING TIME: 10 MINUTES

FOR THE WHIPPED CREAM

- 1 cup (250 mL) heavy or whipping (35%) cream
- 2 tbsp (15 g) confectioners' (icing) sugar

FOR THE CHESTNUT CREAM

- 1 tbsp (15 g) granulated sugar
- $\frac{1}{4}$ cup (60 mL) heavy or whipping (35%) cream
- $\frac{3}{4}$ cup (110 g) cooked peeled chestnuts

FOR THE CREPES

- $1\frac{2}{3}$ cups (400 mL) crepe batter (see recipe on page 17)
- 3 tbsp (40 g) butter, melted

TIP

IF THE CHESTNUT CREAM IS TOO THICK TO SPREAD, ADD A LITTLE WATER.

HOW TO FOLD

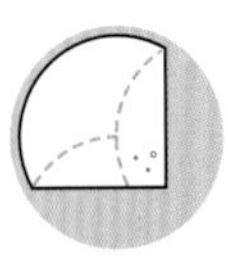

CHESTNUT CREAM CREPE

WITH WHIPPED CREAM

Make the whipped cream: Pour the cream into a chilled bowl and add the confectioners' sugar. Whip until the cream forms medium peaks. Set aside.

Make the chestnut cream: In a saucepan, dissolve the sugar in the cream over low heat. In a blender, purée the chestnuts with the sugar-cream mixture until smooth. Set aside.

Heat the crepe maker to 430°F (220°C) (or the skillet) and grease as directed. Pour and spread one-quarter (about $6\frac{1}{2}$ tbsp/100 mL) of the batter evenly. Cook, flipping the crepe, as directed. Brush the crepe with some of the melted butter. Use the spatula to fold the crepe into a fan shape, then serve it folded side down on a plate.

Repeat the above steps for the other 3 crepes.

For each crepe, spread one-quarter of the chestnut cream in the center. Make a quenelle of whipped cream with a 1 tablespoon (15 mL) measure and place it in the center of the crepe.

Fig Crepe

with Spiced Salted Caramel

MAKES 4 CREPES
Preparation: 20 minutes
Cooking time: 25 minutes

FOR THE SPICED SALTED CARAMEL

- $\frac{1}{4}$ cup (60 mL) heavy or whipping (35%) cream
- 3 tbsp + 1 tsp (50 g) salted butter
- 6 tbsp (80 g) granulated sugar
- $\frac{3}{4}$ cup + 5 tsp (200 mL) water
- $\frac{1}{2}$ tsp (1 g) gingerbread spices

SAUTÉED FIGS

- 4 fresh figs (about $5\frac{1}{3}$ oz/160 g)
- 1 tbsp (14 g) butter

FOR THE CREPES

- $1\frac{2}{3}$ cups (400 mL) crepe batter (see recipe on page 17)
- 3 tbsp (40 g) butter, melted

TIPS

TO COOK THE FIGS, COOK THEM QUICKLY ON BOTH SIDES OVER HIGH HEAT, THEN REMOVE FROM THE HEAT.

STORE EXTRA SPICED SALTED CARAMEL IN A JAR IN THE REFRIGERATOR FOR UP TO 1 MONTH.

HOW TO FOLD

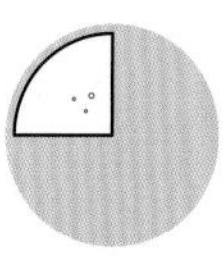

Make the spiced salted caramel: Warm the cream in a saucepan over low heat. In another saucepan, melt the butter. Add the sugar and water to the butter, stirring well. Over high heat, cook until a soft caramel forms. Stir and watch for splattering. Remove the saucepan from the heat. Add the warm cream and stir well. Stir in the spices. Set aside.

Prepare the sautéed figs: Cut the figs into fifths, then sauté the pieces in a skillet in butter over high heat. Set aside.

Heat the crepe maker to 430°F (220°C) (or the skillet) and grease as directed. Pour and spread one-quarter (about $6\frac{1}{2}$ tbsp/100 mL) of the batter evenly. Cook, flipping the crepe, as directed. Brush the crepe with some of the melted butter. Use the spatula to fold the crepe into quarters, then serve on a plate.

Repeat the above steps for the other 3 crepes.

Place 5 of the fig pieces on each crepe and pour spiced salted caramel to taste in the center.

Like crepes, cider is part of Breton gastronomic heritage. It is the legacy of a local biodiversity, thanks to a wide variety of apples offering a rich palette of flavors that can be paired with buckwheat and wheat.

From the beginning, Breizh Café has defined itself as a creperie concept but also as a cider bar with the tagline "Le cidre autrement" (cider in fresh ways). At Atelier de la Crêpe, cider has an important place in the training process, with students learning how to pair a galette or crepe with a Breton cider.

Port of Saint-Malo (left) and Terre Nueve quay (right)

WINTER RECIPES

MAKES 4 GALETTES
PREPARATION: 20 MINUTES
COOKING TIME: 30 MINUTES

- 1 potato (about 7 oz/210 g)
- 2 cups (500 mL) galette batter (see recipe on page 15)
- 3 tbsp (40 g) butter, melted
- $\frac{1}{3}$ cup (80 g) crème fraîche
- 1 cup + 6 tbsp (160 g) grated raclette cheese
- 3 oz (90 g) thinly sliced cured ham or prosciutto

HOW TO FOLD

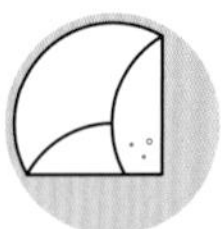

Raclette Cheese and Ham Galette

with Potatoes and Crème Fraîche

Prepare the potato: Cook the potato in a saucepan of boiling salted water for 20 minutes. Drain and cut the potato into $\frac{1}{2}$-inch (1 cm) thick slices.

Heat the crepe maker to 480°F (250°C) (or the skillet) and grease as directed. Pour and spread $\frac{1}{2}$ cup (125 mL) of the batter evenly. Brush the surface of the galette with some of the melted butter. Add one-quarter each of the potato slices, crème fraîche and cheese, then cook. When the edges start to lift, use the spatula to fold the galette into a fan shape. Brush the folded edges of the galette with melted butter.

Remove the galette from the crepe maker (or skillet) and serve it on a plate.

Repeat the above steps for the other 3 galettes.

Top each galette with one-quarter of the ham.

MAKES 4 GALETTES
PREPARATION: 30 MINUTES
COOKING TIME: 40 MINUTES

FOR THE MUSTARD SAUCE

- 2/3 cup (150 mL) heavy or whipping (35%) cream
- 5 tsp (20 g) whole-grain mustard
- 1 tbsp (15 g) Dijon mustard

FOR THE BRAISED CABBAGE

- 1 lb 10 oz (800 g) cabbage
- 1 tbsp (15 g) butter
- 1 1/2 tsp (8 g) fine salt
- 2/3 cup (150 mL) dry cider

FOR THE GALETTES

- 4 farmers' sausages
- 2 cups (500 mL) galette batter (see recipe on page 15)
- 3 tbsp (40 g) butter, melted

HOW TO FOLD

Braised Cabbage Galette

with Sausage and Whole-Grain Mustard Sauce

Make the mustard sauce: Heat the cream in a saucepan on medium heat. Add the two mustards and mix well, then simmer until slightly reduced. Set aside.

Prepare the cabbage: Slice the cabbage thinly. In a skillet, melt the butter. Add the cabbage and salt. Stir. Add the cider. Cover and simmer over low heat for 20 minutes, until the cabbage is tender. Remove the lid and let the liquid evaporate. Set aside.

Cook the sausages in the skillet. Cut them into thick slices.

Heat the crepe maker to 480°F (250°C) (or the skillet) and grease as directed. Pour and spread 1/2 cup (125 mL) of the batter evenly. Brush the galette with some of the melted butter. Place one-quarter of the braised cabbage in the center and cook. When the edges start to lift, use the spatula to fold the galette into an open triangle. Brush the folded edges of the galette with melted butter.

Remove the galette from the crepe maker (or skillet) and serve it on a plate.

Repeat the above steps for the other 3 galettes.

Arrange one-quarter of the sliced sausages on top of each galette and drizzle with mustard sauce.

MAKES 4 GALETTES
PREPARATION: 15 MINUTES
COOKING TIME: 25 MINUTES

FOR THE LEEK FONDUE

- $1^3/_4$ lb (850 g) leeks (3 to 4 large)
- 7 tbsp (100 g) butter
- 2 tsp (10 g) fine salt
- 6 tbsp + 2 tsp (100 mL) heavy or whipping (35%) cream

FOR THE GALETTES

- 2 cups (500 mL) galette batter (see recipe on page 15)
- 3 tbsp (40 g) butter, melted
- 5 oz (150 g) smoked salmon, sliced

TIP

TO WASH THE LEEKS, USE WHITE VINEGAR. RINSE WELL, THEN DRAIN USING A SALAD SPINNER.

HOW TO FOLD

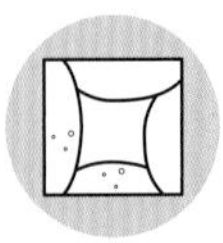

Smoked Salmon and Leek Fondue Galette

Make the leek fondue: Peel and trim the leeks, then cut them into large pieces. Rinse them several times to remove all the dirt. In a saucepan, melt the butter on high heat. Add the leeks and salt; cook over low heat for 15 minutes. Add the cream and simmer, stirring, until the liquid has evaporated. Set aside.

Heat the crepe maker to 480°F (250°C) (or the skillet) and grease as directed. Pour and spread $^1/_2$ cup (125 mL) of the batter evenly. Brush the galette with some of the melted butter. Place one-quarter of the leek fondue in the center and cook 1 minute. Add one-quarter of the smoked salmon. When the edges start to lift, use the spatula to fold the galette into an open square (full fold). Brush the folded edges of the galette with melted butter.

Remove the galette from the crepe maker (or skillet) and serve it on a plate.

Repeat the above steps for the other 3 galettes.

MAKES 4 GALETTES
PREPARATION: 30 MINUTES
COOKING TIME: 35 MINUTES

ENDIVE FONDUE, SMOKED BACON AND REBLOCHON GALETTE

WITH CREAM SAUCE

FOR THE ENDIVE FONDUE

- 2 lbs (1 kg) Belgian endives (about 5 heads)
- 3 tbsp (40 g) butter
- $1\frac{1}{2}$ tsp (8 g) fine salt
- $\frac{1}{2}$ tsp (2 g) superfine granulated sugar

FOR THE CREAM SAUCE

- $\frac{3}{4}$ cup + 5 tsp (200 mL) heavy or whipping (35%) cream
- Superfine granulated sugar (if needed)
- 1 tsp (5 g) butter
- 1 tsp (4 g) all-purpose flour

FOR THE GALETTES

- 4 oz (125 g) sliced smoked bacon
- 2 cups (500 mL) galette batter (see recipe on page 15)
- 3 tbsp (40 g) butter, melted
- 5 oz (150 g) Reblochon cheese, thinly sliced

HOW TO FOLD

Prepare the endive fondue: Cut the endives into $\frac{3}{4}$-inch (2 cm) thick slices. Melt the butter in a saucepan over low heat. Add the endives, salt and sugar. Cover and cook, stirring occasionally. The endives will release a lot of liquid. Reserve $\frac{3}{4}$ cup (175 mL) of the liquid in a saucepan and drain the rest. Set the endives aside separately.

Make the cream sauce: Heat the reserved endive liquid on high. Boil until reduced by half. Add the cream. Taste the sauce. If it is still slightly bitter, add a little sugar. In another saucepan, heat the butter, add the flour and cook, stirring, for 1 minute. Whisk this roux into the sauce until smooth. Cook, stirring, until slightly thickened. Set aside.

Fry the smoked bacon in a skillet or on a plancha.

Heat the crepe maker to 480°F (250°C) (or a skillet) and grease as directed. Pour and spread $\frac{1}{2}$ cup (125 mL) of the batter evenly. Brush the galette with some of the melted butter. Place one-quarter of the endives in the center. Add one-quarter of the Reblochon cheese and cook. When the edges start to lift, spoon one-quarter of the cream sauce in the center. Use the spatula to fold the galette into an open square (full fold). Brush the folded edges of the galette with melted butter. Cook until the cheese is melted.

Remove the galette from the crepe maker (or skillet) and serve it on a plate.

Repeat the above steps for the other 3 galettes.

Top each galette with one-quarter of the bacon.

MAKES 4 GALETTES

PREPARATION: 15 MINUTES

COOKING TIME: 40 MINUTES

FOR THE CREAMED CHICKEN WITH MUSTARD

- 1 lb (500 g) boneless skinless chicken breasts
- 1 tbsp (15 mL) sunflower oil
- Salt
- Pepper
- 3/4 cup (175 mL) dry cider
- 1 cup (130 g) chopped onions
- 8 oz (250 g) button mushrooms, finely chopped
- 5 tsp (20 g) Dijon mustard
- 1 cup (250 mL) heavy or whipping (35%) cream

FOR THE GALETTES

- 2 cups (500 mL) galette batter (see recipe on page 15)
- 3 tbsp (40 g) butter, melted
- 1 cup (120 g) grated Emmental cheese

TIP

BE SURE TO SPRINKLE THE EMMENTAL OVER THE WHOLE GALETTE SO IT DOESN'T TEAR WHEN YOU SERVE IT ON THE PLATE.

HOW TO FOLD

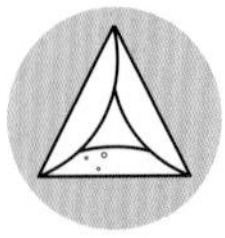

Creamed Chicken, Onion and Mustard Galette

Prepare the creamed chicken: Cut the chicken into large chunks. In a skillet, over high heat, brown the chicken in the oil. Season with salt and pepper. Cook the chicken until it's no longer pink inside. Set aside. Using the same skillet, add the cider and boil over high heat until reduced by half, scraping the bottom of the pan to deglaze. Over low heat, add the onions and mushrooms and cook for 20 minutes until very soft. Stir in the mustard and cream, add the chicken and stir until heated through.

Heat the crepe maker to 480°F (250°C) (or the skillet) and grease as directed. Pour and spread 1/2 cup (125 mL) of the batter evenly. Brush the galette with some of the melted butter. Sprinkle one-quarter of the Emmental over the galette, add one-quarter of the creamed chicken and cook. When the edges start to lift, use the spatula to fold the galette into an open triangle. Brush the folded edges of the galette with melted butter.

Remove the galette from the crepe maker (or skillet) and serve it on a plate.

Repeat the above steps for the other 3 galettes.

Mashed Carrot, Cumin, Cilantro and Shrimp Galette

MAKES 4 GALETTES
Preparation: 20 MINUTES
Cooking time: 50 MINUTES

FOR THE MASHED CARROTS

- 14 oz (435 g) carrots
- 3 tbsp (40 g) butter
- 3 tbsp (45 mL) heavy or whipping (35%) cream
- 4 tsp (4 g) chopped fresh cilantro leaves
- 1 tsp (2 g) ground cumin

FOR THE ORANGE AND CIDER SAUCE

- 2 cups + 6 tbsp (590 mL) orange juice
- 2 cups + 6 tbsp (590 mL) dry cider
- $\frac{1}{4}$ cup (60 g) butter

FOR THE GALETTES

- 16 medium shrimp
- 2 cups (500 mL) galette batter (see recipe on page 15)
- 4 tbsp (60 g) butter, melted, divided
- 4 small carrots with greens

Make the mashed carrots: Peel the carrots and cook them in boiling water. Drain and mash with the butter and cream. Add the cilantro to the mash with the cumin. Mix well. Set aside.

Make the orange and cider sauce: Pour the orange juice and cider into a saucepan. Boil over high heat until reduced and thickened. Stir in the butter. Set aside.

Sauté the shrimp in a skillet with 1 tbsp (15 g) of the butter.

Heat the crepe maker to 480°F (250°C) (or the skillet) and grease as directed. Pour and spread $\frac{1}{2}$ cup (125 mL) of the batter evenly. Brush the galette with some of the remaining melted butter. Place one-quarter of the mashed carrots in the center and cook. When the edges start to lift, use the spatula to fold the galette into a closed rectangle.

Remove the galette from the crepe maker (or skillet) and serve it folded side down on a plate.

Repeat the above steps for the other 3 galettes.

Peel the small carrots. Place 1 carrot down one side of each galette. Place 4 shrimp on top of each galette. Drizzle 2 tbsp (30 mL) of the orange and cider sauce on the plate next to the galette.

TIPS

YOU CAN ALSO SERVE THE GALETTE WITH LOBSTER.

EXTRA ORANGE AND CIDER SAUCE CAN BE STORED IN A JAR IN THE REFRIGERATOR FOR UP TO 1 MONTH.

HOW TO FOLD

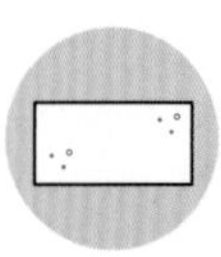

Almond Cream Crepe

with Toasted Almonds

MAKES 4 CREPES
PREPARATION: 20 MINUTES
COOKING TIME: 20 MINUTES
RESTING TIME: 30 MINUTES IN THE FRIDGE

FOR THE ALMOND CREAM

- 14 tbsp (200 g) butter (at room temperature)
- 1 cup (200 g) superfine granulated sugar
- 4 pasteurized eggs
- 2 cups (200 g) ground almonds

FOR THE CREPES

- $\frac{2}{3}$ cup (60 g) sliced almonds
- $1\frac{2}{3}$ cups (400 mL) crepe batter (see recipe on page 17)
- 3 tbsp (40 g) butter, melted

TIPS

FOR A MORE DECADENT DESSERT, SERVE WITH CHOCOLATE SAUCE!

THIS RECIPE CONTAINS A RAW EGG. IF YOU ARE CONCERNED ABOUT THE FOOD SAFETY OF RAW EGG, SUBSTITUTE PASTEURIZED EGG IN THE SHELL OR $\frac{1}{4}$ CUP (60 ML) PASTEURIZED LIQUID WHOLE EGG.

HOW TO FOLD

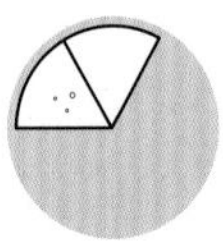

Make the almond cream: In a bowl, mix the softened butter with the sugar using a flexible spatula. Add the eggs and mix well. Add the ground almonds and stir. Cover and refrigerate for 30 minutes.

Preheat the oven to 350°F (180°C). Place the sliced almonds on a baking sheet and toast until golden, stirring occasionally. Set aside.

Heat the crepe maker to 430°F (220°C) (or the skillet) and grease as directed. Pour and spread one-quarter (about $6\frac{1}{2}$ tbsp/100 mL) of the batter evenly. Cook, flipping the crepe, as directed. Brush the crepe with some of the melted butter. Add a scant $\frac{1}{4}$ cup (40 g) of the almond cream, then fold the crepe into quarters, partially folding the right side over the left side. Serve the crepe on a plate.

Repeat the above steps for the other 3 crepes.

Brush each crepe with melted butter and sprinkle with one-quarter of the toasted almonds.

MAKES 4 CREPES

PREPARATION: 30 MINUTES
COOKING TIME: 25 MINUTES
RESTING TIME: 1 NIGHT IN THE FRIDGE
BAKING TIME: 3 TO 5 HOURS

FOR THE CANDIED ORANGES

- 1 orange
- 3 tbsp (45 mL) water
- $\frac{1}{4}$ cup (50 g) granulated sugar

FOR THE ORANGE BUTTER

- 2 tbsp (25 g) superfine granulated sugar
- 2 tsp (10 mL) water
- Zest and juice of 1 orange
- 2 tsp (10 mL) lemon juice
- $\frac{1}{3}$ cup (80 g) butter

FOR THE CREPES

- $1\frac{2}{3}$ cups (400 mL) crepe batter (see recipe on page 17)
- 3 tbsp (40 g) butter, melted
- 4 scoops vanilla ice cream

TIP

FOR THE RIGHT CONSISTENCY OF ORANGE BUTTER, MAKE SURE THE MIXTURE HAS REDUCED WELL BEFORE ADDING THE BUTTER.

HOW TO FOLD

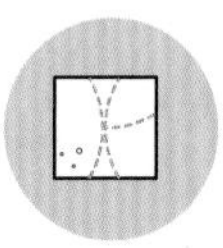

ORANGE BUTTER AND CANDIED ORANGE CREPE

WITH VANILLA ICE CREAM

The day before, make the candied oranges: Cut the orange into $\frac{1}{4}$-inch (5 mm) thick slices. Boil the water and sugar in a saucepan until the sugar dissolves. Add the orange and remove from heat. Cover and let the orange slices sit in the liquid overnight at room temperature.

The day of serving, make the orange butter: In a saucepan, combine the sugar and the water. Boil over high heat until the sugar starts to caramelize. Add the orange juice and lemon juice. Simmer over low heat until reduced to a syrup. Add the orange zest and the butter to the saucepan and mix well. Let cool, then chill in the fridge. Melt gently before using.

Meanwhile, preheat the oven to 195°F (90°C). Drain the candied orange slices and place them in a single layer on a parchment paper–lined baking sheet. Bake until the slices are dried. This could take anywhere from 3 to 5 hours depending on how juicy the oranges are.

Heat the crepe maker to 430°F (220°C) (or the skillet) and grease as directed. Pour and spread one-quarter (about $6\frac{1}{2}$ tbsp/100 mL) of the batter evenly. Cook, flipping the crepe, as directed. Brush the crepe with some of the orange butter. Use the spatula to fold the crepe into a square and serve it folded side down on a plate.

Repeat the above steps for the other 3 crepes.

Drizzle each crepe with a little orange butter and place a scoop of ice cream on top. Add a slice of candied orange.

MAKES 4 CREPES
PREPARATION: 15 MINUTES
COOKING TIME: 15 MINUTES

FOR THE CHOCOLATE-CARAMEL SPREAD

- $^{1}/_{4}$ cup (45 g) chopped dark chocolate
- $^{1}/_{3}$ cup (100 g) sweetened condensed milk
- $2^{1}/_{2}$ tbsp (40 g) salted caramel (see recipe page 36)

FOR THE CREPES

- $1^{2}/_{3}$ cups (400 mL) crepe batter (see recipe on page 17)
- 3 tbsp (40 g) butter, melted

TIP

YOU CAN MAKE ROLLS WITH THIS CREPE. TO DO THIS, MAKE THE CREPES AHEAD OF TIME AND CHILL THEM BEFORE ASSEMBLING.

HOW TO FOLD

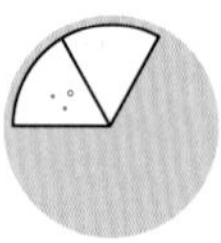

Crepe with Homemade Chocolate-Caramel Spread

Make the chocolate-caramel spread: Place the chocolate in a heatproof bowl set over a saucepan of hot water to melt. Place the milk and salted caramel in a bowl. Stir in the melted chocolate, mixing well until smooth.

Heat the crepe maker to 430°F (220°C) (or the skillet) and grease as directed. Pour and spread one-quarter (about $6^{1}/_{2}$ tbsp/100 mL) of the batter evenly. Cook, flipping the crepe, as directed. Brush the crepe with some of the melted butter. Use the spatula to fold the crepe into quarters, partially folding the right side over the left side, then serve it on a plate.

Repeat the above steps for the other 3 crepes. Brush the crepes with melted butter and dollop each with one-quarter of the chocolate-caramel spread.

MAKES 4 CREPES
PREPARATION: 30 MINUTES
COOKING TIME: 35 MINUTES

FOR THE TATIN-STYLE APPLES

- $2\frac{1}{2}$ apples (1 lb/500 g)
- 6 tbsp + 2 tsp (100 g) butter
- 1 cup (200 g) granulated sugar
- 6 tbsp + 2 tsp (100 mL) apple juice

FOR THE BUCKWHEAT CRUMBLE

- 3 tbsp (25 g) buckwheat flour
- $\frac{1}{4}$ cup (35 g) all-purpose flour
- 2 tbsp + 1 tsp (35 g) butter (at room temperature)
- 2 tbsp (25 g) brown sugar

FOR THE CREPES

- $1\frac{2}{3}$ cups (400 mL) crepe batter (see recipe on page 17)
- 3 tbsp (40 g) butter, melted

TIP

FOR A MORE DECADENT CREPE, ADD A SCOOP OF VANILLA ICE CREAM.

HOW TO FOLD

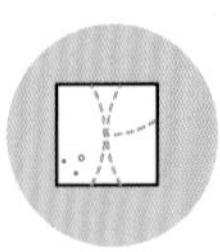

Tatin-Style Apple Crepe

Prepare the apples: Peel and core the apples, and cut each full apple into 8 even wedges, and the half apple into 4 wedges. In a skillet, melt the butter over high heat and add the apples. Add the sugar and caramelize the apple pieces on both sides. Add the juice to stop the caramelization. Set aside.

Prepare the crumble: Preheat the oven to 350°F (180°C). Mix the two flours in a bowl. Add the softened butter and sugar and mix well until you get a sandy consistency. Spread the mixture on a baking sheet and bake for 20 minutes. Set aside.

Heat the crepe maker to 430°F (220°C) (or the skillet) and grease as directed. Pour and spread one-quarter (about $6\frac{1}{2}$ tbsp/100 mL) of the batter evenly. Cook, flipping the crepe, as directed. Brush the crepe with some of the melted butter. Use the spatula to fold the crepe into a closed square and serve it folded side down on a plate.

Repeat the above steps for the other 3 crepes.

Brush the crepes with melted butter. For each crepe, place 5 pieces of caramelized apple on top (if they are cold, reheat them first), then drizzle with one-quarter of the juice. Sprinkle one-quarter of the crumble on top of the apples.

INDEX

E

F

G

H

I

L

M

N

O

Thank you to the Brittany Region and the City of Saint-Malo for their support of the Atelier de la Crêpe educational project.

Mastering Authentic Crepes & Galettes

Library and Archives Canada Cataloguing in Publication
Title: Mastering authentic crepes & galettes / Bertrand Larcher, founder of Breizh Café.
Other titles: Atelier de la crêpe. English | Mastering authentic crepes and galettes
Names: Larcher, Bertrand, 1966- author.
Description: Translation of: Atelier de la crêpe : Saint-Malo : devenez un pro des crêpes et des galettes. | Includes index.
Identifiers: Canadiana 20240349822 | ISBN 9780778807209 (softcover)
Subjects: LCSH: Pancakes, waffles, etc. | LCGFT: Cookbooks.
Classification: LCC TX770.P34 L3713 2024 | DDC 641.81/53—dc23

Design: Nicole Dassonville
Layout and Production: PageWave Graphics Inc.
Editors: Jennifer MacKenzie/Amy Treadwell
Proofreader: Kelly Jones
Translator: Anne Louise Mahoney
Indexer: Gillian Watts
Photography: Emanuela Cino

We acknowledge the support of the Government of Canada.
Canadä

Published by Robert Rose Inc.
120 Eglinton Avenue East, Suite 800, Toronto, Ontario, Canada M4P 1E2
Tel: (416) 322-6552 Fax: (416) 322-6936
www.robertrose.ca

Printed and bound in China

1 2 3 4 5 6 7 8 9 ESP 32 31 30 29 28 27 26 25 24